W9-BYZ-823

HORSE COLOR EXPLAINED

A BREEDER'S PERSPECTIVE

Jeanette Gower

Trafalgar Square Publishing

Dedication

To my family for their patience and support.

First published in the United States of America in 2000 by
Trafalgar Square Publishing, North Pomfret, Vermont 05053

Printed in Hong Kong through Colorcraft Ltd

© Jeanette Gower, 1999

All rights reserved. No part of this publication may be reproduced,
stored in a retrieval system, or transmitted, in any form or by any
means, electronic, mechanical, photocopying, recording or otherwise,
without the prior permission of the publisher in writing.

Library of Congress
Catalog Card Number: 00-100531

ISBN 1-57076-162-0

Set in Sabon 9.5/11

10 9 8 7 6 5 4 3 2

CONTENTS

ACKNOWLEDGMENTS

This book has been a 20-year project. Thanks in particular go to my husband, Peter, who encouraged me to write and lecture on horse colour, when in the early days I lacked confidence in what I considered to be my limited experience and expertise. Ultimately I realised that other writers also had limitations because so little was known. There followed an exciting adventure into the mysteries of horse colour genetics. Thanks to Peter also for his beautiful colour photos which I believe are second to none; and for allowing me the space to write this book between the pressures of juggling family life, work and study commitments.

Thank you to my daughter Kim and my father Alan for their enthusiastic input.

Thanks also to: Don Burke, Dot Childs, Jo Heard, Leanne Millard and Keith Stevens without whose help and encouragement this book would not have happened.

I also appreciate assistance from N. Arthur, S. Batteate, S. Dolling, D. Hill, B. Kincade, P. Lee, B. Page, M. Lund, V. and S. McAuliffe, C. Rogers, M. van Bon, J. and B. von Raalte, K. Szalay, J. Wiersema, R. Wilkerson and L. Young.

Thanks to Ian Pickett (Senior Lecturer DETAFE Equine Studies), my students and fellow breeders, who have provided immense feedback over the years and stimulated me with difficult questions.

Thanks to my editor Anne Savage for her enthusiasm—we clicked right away.

And finally, a very special thank you to Albert.

A note on the photographs used

With few exceptions the photographs have been professionally taken. Some have been supplied by the owners. Every attempt has been made to show horses that are good representatives of their breeds. The horses have been photographed in top coat condition so as to reflect the correctness of colour. Horses 'out of coat' may be misleading as they frequently change shade or 'colour up' to their true colour later.

It is not within the scope of this book to show examples of every different shade. However, if you know of a horse whose colour does not appear, the author would be interested to hear about it.

A note on the terminology used

As far as possible, horsemen's terms have been used rather than academic terminology, with a corresponding degree of technical licence in the explanations. Where terminology is not defined in the text, the reader should refer to the glossary at the end of this book. The term 'horse*man*' is used for simplicity and with non-sexist intent, as the contribution and participation of women in all facets of horsemanship and horse breeding is well known and highly regarded.

FOREWORD

Jeanette Gower has spent over 20 years researching the aspects of coat colour inheritance in horses and her work is truly outstanding. No longer will colour inheritance be luck of the draw. Master this book and you will know exactly what foals you will get in exactly which proportions.

For the modern responsible horse breeder, a new era is at hand. How can you breed 100 per cent palomino foals? How can you breed jet black foals? Will your paints produce lethal whites? Is a taffy a palomino? These and many more questions are answered herein.

This is a very important book. Horse breeders all over the world are spending a lot of time

Catch a Bird, a unique striped Thoroughbred (see Case Study and colour photo on page 64)

researching the science of horse genetics. Tremendous advances have occurred recently and this book is state of the art. In the past, the science of genetics of horse breeding was particularly backward, when compared to that of other domestic animals such as poultry, dogs, cats and budgerigars. Breeding for preferred coat colour has produced much misery for the horses themselves. Due to a lack of understanding of the genes involved, well-intentioned paint breeders, for example, have produced 'lethal whites'—that is, pure white foals that die in agony soon after birth. These things can now be avoided.

I have been involved in genetics for about 40 years. I studied it at university and TAFE and have lectured on the subject at various breed clubs. I can honestly say that Jeanette Gower is one of the finest geneticists that I have met and reading this book was a real pleasure.

Whenever I read books on breeding of most animals, I find they contain errors and all too often the work is dated and fails to conform to the basic science of heredity. Bringing together years of observation and her wealth of experience as a hands-on horse breeder, Jeanette has avoided the errors of other authors. So relax, and savour the book, it can save you a lot of heartache.

For the record I have been using Jeanette's insights to breed my own horses and every time the foals turn out as she predicts. I bless the day I met her.

Don Burke
1999

PREFACE

We are all colour blind. We all have biases and subjective views on the merits or otherwise of certain colours, our favourite colours or our most disliked colours. If you disagree, just ask yourself if you would be prepared to own a horse that is colour X? (Insert chestnut, albino, pinto, spotted, grey or whatever is your personal dislike.) Moreover, if you had to pay top money for it, would you buy a horse of that colour? Would you risk the 'wrong' colour for the show ring? Would you buy a Pinto if you were aiming for the Dressage World Championships or the Olympic Games? Would breeding certain colours prove to be unprofitable?

And what of the various theories about how certain colours are produced? There are many, which have varying degrees of merit. Perhaps the reader has some knowledge of colour inheritance and has lost the ability to be open-minded on the subject, because of a favourite theory. The trouble is foals don't read books; some don't fit the theories. When an unexpected colour is produced, we discredit theory or disbelieve what we see. Because of colour blindness, some owners incorrectly register their horse, or fail to correct the errors of colour registration of a previous owner. Some stud books register the colour as the one the horse 'ought' to be based on outdated information, and consequently any mess must be sorted out by blood testing and the like.

For the past 25 years I have been exploring colour inheritance in horses. My interest started at the age of 16, when I put my first mare in foal. In spite of contacting various experienced breeders, there was no consensus of opinion as to what colour foal I should expect. I had bred pigeons previously and knew that the colour inheritance of pigeons was reasonably well established. Indeed most pigeon breeders had a comprehensive knowledge of this subject. I was amazed to find that my enquiries with horse breeders led me absolutely nowhere. Breeders generally had no concept of the science of heredity and there was no reliable literature on the subject. Furthermore, I discovered many horse colour researchers were academics who used a minefield of terminology and spent little time out in the field actually looking at horses or talking to breeders. Colour inheritance theory was therefore a confusing conglomeration of myth, contradictory evidence and terminology, inaccuracy and gobbledygook.

I discovered that colour inheritance in horses, far from being complex, is actually quite simple. Since I failed chemistry, and had a low pass in mathematics, I can honestly inform you that you don't need to be a genius to acquire the knowledge that I have gained over these years. In fact, after reading this book I sincerely believe you will experience the joy of discovering how simple horse colour genetics really is, and will find reward in being able to answer your own questions. I suggest you read over passages of interest several times—each time the message will become clearer.

I have included some of my own theories for you to consider, because geneticists have a long way to go before there is a complete understanding of colour in horses. I would appreciate any feedback you have. Who knows? I might have to rewrite this book as a result.

Jeanette Gower

PART 1

BASIC INHERITANCE

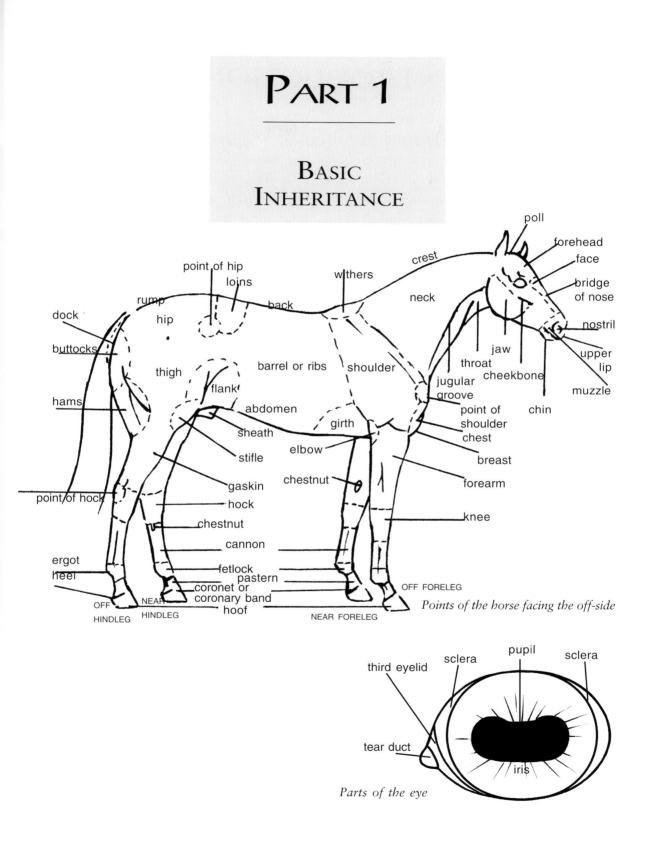

Points of the horse facing the off-side

point of hip
loins
rump
back
withers
crest
neck
poll
forehead
face
bridge of nose
nostril
upper lip
muzzle
chin
dock
hip
jaw
throat
cheekbone
jugular groove
point of shoulder
chest
breast
forearm
knee
buttocks
thigh
barrel or ribs
shoulder
hams
flank
abdomen
sheath
girth
elbow
stifle
chestnut
point of hock
gaskin
hock
chestnut
cannon
ergot
heel
fetlock
pastern
coronet or coronary band
hoof
OFF HINDLEG
NEAR HINDLEG
NEAR FORELEG
OFF FORELEG

Parts of the eye

third eyelid
sclera
pupil
sclera
tear duct
iris

INTRODUCTION

Is horse breeding a science or a game of chance?

Racehorse breeders believe in the value of a pedigree and search for a preponderance of black type or major stakeswinners. Buyers look at the bloodlines and relationships to winners in each family and select their purchase on pedigree. Yet this does not guarantee a winner. Colour breeders have the difficulty of planning a future mating not only to have the desired pedigree, but also to produce the chosen colour.

We all know that breeding stock which looks magnificent sometimes produces inferior progeny, while some ordinary-looking animals produce excellent offspring. There are also cases of horses which look normal but produce offspring with lethal defects. The basis for most effective breeding programs has proven to be inbreeding, yet performance horse enthusiasts crossbreed with the Thoroughbred. Few crossbreds make it, however, as breeding stock.

All of this serves to leave the average horse breeder and buyer very confused. So far, it looks as though breeding *is* a game of chance. But there is also a scientific approach. Genetics is the science of heredity. Genetic material is passed on from generation to generation. These genetic materials, or units of inheritance, are loosely referred to by breeders as 'genes'. Genes are passed on to the next generation in accordance with the principles of probability and the resultant characteristics are a combination of a horse's genes, as well as its environment. Yet the average horseperson's understanding of the principles of genetics is fuzzy.

This book aims to introduce you to some of the principles of genetics in a most basic way. Do not fear. Genetics is logic, and colour breeding is using your powers of observation in a logical way. Many of these observations have already been made by experienced breeders using expertise gained over a period of years in the industry. But these breeders will tell you that they have made a lot of mistakes along the way, and that any books on genetics they have studied only serve to confuse, due to the lack of agreement by geneticists in many areas, and the

apparent lack of consultation between horse geneticists and breeders. The difficulties are increased by the gaps or inaccuracies in the stud records of previous owners and the unreliability of association studbooks.

The great horse breeders of the past were unknowingly using genetic principles when they made breeding decisions based on their uncanny powers of observation and logic. They were prepared to cull ruthlessly because of the need to breed the best type of horse to serve man. Modern stud owners tend to breed for pleasure, a tax break or investment, and mostly have outside income sources to maintain their hobby. This means that culling is frequently ignored in favour of keeping a horse with a single desired requirement. This particularly occurs with colour breeding, where selection for temperament and conformation often takes second place to producing the required colour.

With little background knowledge, the would-be investor sees colour as the goal. Colour breeding is very mysterious to him and very hard to achieve. However, colour alone does not constitute good breeding stock. Only when the breeder finds out that failures hit his pocket hard will he realise that basic genetics is a valuable tool for his endeavours. A knowledge of the mechanisms of inheritance and the basis of colour will afford a greater success rate in achieving a colour goal, leaving the investor to get on with the job of selecting for quality, temperament and ability. An understanding of colour inheritance has the added advantage of introducing the breeder in the simplest possible way to the general principles of genetics, thus enabling use of genetics in the more complex and important areas of temperament improvement and performance.

Successful horse breeders use logic and objectivity. They have an ability to see the overall picture, carefully formulating goals based on knowledge and experience, culling ruthlessly. They realise that horse breeding, more particularly than breeding with other livestock, is a long-term project.

1

HORSE BREEDING AND GENETICS

Genetic material is rather like beads on a string, strung along the chromosomes; in the case of horses, along 32 pairs of chromosomes in each cell. Each bead or gene normally exists in the same place on the same chromosome. These positions, or sites, are called the genetic loci. At any locus, one of a series of *alleles* may be found. Alleles are alternate genes at identical sites on the chromosomes. As the loci are paired (one locus being on each of a pair of chromosomes), each horse has two allelic genes present from those available in the series (Figure 1.1). A series refers to all the alleles possible for a characteristic such as eye colour; alleles of this series might control brown, blue, grey, green or glass eye.

The maximum number of alleles that may be available in a series for any species is unknown, but in the case of humans, 90 different alleles at one locus have been found. In horses, two alleles for any one characteristic, such as dun colour and non-dun colour, is the norm.

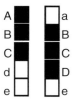

FIGURE **1.1** *Example of chromosomes with pairs of alleles at five loci:*
    three pairs are the same (BB, CC, ee)
    two pairs are different (Aa, dD)

The genes may be described as programs carried by the DNA molecules of each cell which determine the kind of products the cell will manufacture. For instance, it could be blood type, hoof density, eye or hair colour. This process is the basis of life.

If the cells do not manufacture the right things at the right time in the right place, living may be impaired, abortion may occur soon after conception, or the foal may die. It is important then that the message imparted by the genes comes across loud and clear. This is a simple process if the alleles

at each paired locus are the same, for each gives the same message. But what happens if they are different? For example, at the dun colour locus *D* in the horse, the unmatched alleles would be for dun and non-dun.

Each allele then gives a conflicting message and somehow this conflict must be resolved.

SIMPLE MENDELIAN INHERITANCE

The simplest way this difficulty is overcome, is if one gene completely overshadows the message of the other, masking it, as if it were not even there. A masking gene is known as the *dominant* allele, while the gene that is hidden is known as the *recessive* allele. Such action is known as Mendelian inheritance, named after the Austrian monk, Gregor Mendel (1822–84). His study of the hereditary characterics of garden peas led to the publication, in 1866, of papers which explained the transmission of certain traits from one generation to the next.

Peas are an ideal subject for inheritance experiments as they are self-pollinating, that is, the mother and father are one and the same, ensuring exactly the same genetic parentage. Mendel found that when short peas were crossed with tall, the resulting seeds when grown were all tall. Tall was dominant. When these, in turn, self-pollinated, both short and tall progeny resulted. Short plants thus reappeared in the second generation. This led to the eventual proof of the fundamental principle of genetics: genes are not diluted (medium height peas were not produced) or 'lost' in breeding, but are carried on through the population.

Horses which possess different alleles in any gene pair are referred to as *heterozygous* and those which have the same alleles are called *homozygous*. Heterozygous individuals have the genetic blueprint of one masking gene (the dominant gene) and one hidden gene (the recessive gene). Because the recessive gene is hidden, the heterozygous horse will appear outwardly exactly like a homozygous horse.

However, because it is a carrier for the hidden recessive gene the heterozygous horse can *breed* differently. A horse displaying the quality of the recessive gene is always homozygous, since by definition if it were heterozygous, the dominant gene would have been expressed. Such a horse can pass on only a recessive gene; since it is homozygous, it possesses only the recessive gene to pass on.

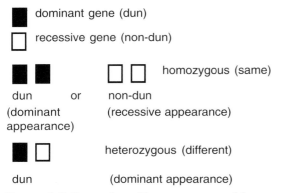

FIGURE 1.2 *Examples of homozygous and heterozygous gene combinations. Two genes; three possible gene combinations*

Where a horse carries a dominant colour gene, unless the horse is homozygous that gene need not be passed on to the next generation, in which case it is eliminated entirely in the progeny and cannot reappear in future generations unless and until it is reintroduced through an outside mating to that colour. For example, dun is a dominant allele. Once the dunning gene is lost from a population, dun cannot reappear until a new dun is introduced to the breeding herd. Why is this the case? Before Mendel published his papers it was known that both males and females contributed characteristics to their offspring, but it was thought that their contributions were somehow mixed or melded together.

When conception takes place:
This is *not* what happens:

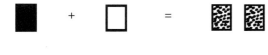

This happens instead:

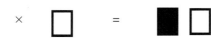

FIGURE 1.3 *When conception takes place (× means 'crossed with')*

That was quite wrong. During reproduction each parent contributes only one allele from its gene pair either to the sperm or to the ovum, each of which has half the number of chromosomes of a normal body cell. In this way, when the sperm and ovum combine, the resulting foal has its full pair of genes again at each locus; the genetic material is passed on paired and 'intact', as indicated in Figure 1.4.

Let us mate a heterozygous sire with a heterozygous dam of the same genetic blueprint. At conception, each parent contributes one of its genes to the offspring and we get four possible combinations (two of which are identical), as shown in Figure 1.4.

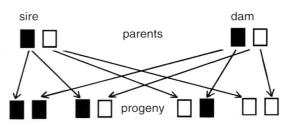

FIGURE 1.4 *Four possible combinations of genes at conception. The arrows show directional pathways.*

The foal will inherit only one of these possible combinations, according to chance. Each is equally likely.

The three points which must be clear are:

- Genes are passed on *intact* from generation to generation;
- It is not the colour which is passed on but the *genes* which produce the colour; and
- Each parent's genetic contribution is *equal*.

The above is not a pedantic notion but fundamental genetic law.

INHERITANCE OF SEX

If you toss a coin, it may come down heads or it may come down tails—there is an equal chance of either. Does this mean that if you toss the coin 1000 times you get 500 heads and 500 tails? No. Does it mean that if you get heads five times in a row you will get tails five times in a row after that? No.

Readers may think this simple enough and it is, but this basic logic rarely seems to be applied to horse breeding. For example, a mare has had five fillies in a row. Does this mean she is a 'filly producer' and the next five foals must be fillies? No, but it is possible. What if a mare has had ten fillies in a row (an unlikely occurrence but it does happen)? Does this mean the next foal will be a colt?

It is no more likely that she will have a filly than a colt, because the chance of the next mating producing a male or female is still 50 per cent and is in no way related to the sex of previous foals.

Determination of sex is made by the combination of the sex chromosomes at conception. Carried in the stallion's sperm cells are female or male sex chromosomes, called X and Y, in equal proportions. The mare carries only X sex chromosomes. It is a matter of chance whether an X or Y sperm cell impregnates the egg of the mare. Like tossing a coin, if it is the Y sperm the foal will be male (XY), if X, the foal will be a filly (XX).

However, there are actually four possible combinations of X and Y chromosomes—XX, XX, YX and YX (as shown in Figure 1.5)—depending on which X chromosome the mare passes on, but obviously two of the combinations are the same, resulting in the probability of equal chances for a colt or filly. Notice this is the probability or chance of a certain result occurring. It does not tell us what the outcome will be, merely what the possibilities are. Like tossing the coin, which we know has an equal chance of being heads or tails, we cannot guarantee which it will be. When we toss the coin again, the previous result will have no bearing at all on the result of the next toss.

The inheritance of sex is an example of chromosome inheritance, where full chromosomes are responsible for the message rather than individual genes, as described previously in the section on simple Mendelian inheritance. There is very little genetic material carried on the Y chromosome, compared with the almost indefinite numbers of genes that can be found on the other 31 chromosomes.

In horses, the few genes on the sex chromosomes are thought by some breeders to influence extremities such as ear length and shape, tail type (thinness, fullness, etc.) and umbilical hernia.

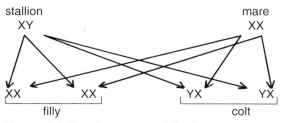

FIGURE 1.5 *Sex chromosome inheritance*

GENETIC LABELLING

In the formulation of certain colours we are generally dealing with individual alleles at a certain locus, although we may be concerned with groups of genes at several series of loci. In most instances we will be dealing with simple Mendelian inheritance. Where a gene at one locus affects the functioning of genes at another locus we say the gene has an *epistatic* effect, that is, it masks the action of genes at another locus. The locus which is masked is said to be *hypostatic*. For example, in horse colour greying is epistatic to the locus for dun/non-dun. In other words, when the greying gene is present at the greying locus it hides/masks the presence of dun/non-dun at the dun locus. The result is a grey horse.

Geneticists by convention label alleles with a simple alphabetical name, which in most instances remains the same from one species to the next, depending on its message. This is similar to the chemist always using O for oxygen, H for hydrogen, and N for nitrogen. It is a universal system. For example, alleles of the *Agouti* series or 'wild colour' (named after a South American rodent), are given the symbol A in all species, and alleles within the series are given a superscript to distinguish them from one another. In the case of the horse, alleles in the *Agouti* series are A^a, A^t, A^A and A^+, in ascending order of dominance. The superscript '+' is always used to denote the 'wild form' or standard of the series, which generally but not always indicates the most frequently occurring allele. Lower case superscripts are used to indicate recessive alleles, upper case is used for the top dominant allele.

The important thing to remember is that in any individual horse, two alleles only can be present on any locus, one on each of a pair of chromosomes. They may be one and the same allele, or they may be two different alleles (as shown in Figure 1.1). For a complete listing of known colour alleles of the horse refer to Table A in Appendix (page 133).

PHENOTYPE AND GENOTYPE

Let us use the example of a grey horse. G^G indicates a grey horse, while G^+ is the wild form, or non-grey. Since we have two alleles at the same locus they can be in the pairs G^GG^G, G^GG^+ or G^+G^+. G^GG^G is different from G^GG^+, but both will indicate a grey horse. A non-grey horse will be G^+G^+.

According to Mendelian law, G^G will override (mask) the recessive G^+ and, with a G^GG^+ genotype, a grey horse will still occur.

A G^GG^+ grey will look exactly like a G^GG^G grey, although its genetic makeup will be different. One, the G^GG^G is homozygous, or pure-breeding, while the other, G^GG^+, is heterozygous, or a carrier individual.

We say that the outward appearance of the two horses is the *phenotype*, and that their phenotype is the same, but the genetic makeup is different. This genetic makeup is known as the *genotype*.

It is important to understand the difference between phenotype and genotype. The first is simply the colour of the horse, and is measurable and observable.

The second is the actual genetic blueprint, the message carried by the genes in the cells. We can't tell what these are entirely, because the recessives are unknown, although we can sometimes gain a fair idea from pedigree research and progeny testing.

Action of colour alleles in the horse
(in ascending order of dominance)

1. *A* from the *Agouti* series influences black (eumelanin) production; 4 probable alleles:
   A^+ restricts black to the points, mane and tail, but makes them indistinct
   A^A also restricts black to the points, mane and tail
   A^t removes black from the soft parts
   A^a has no influence (all black)

2. *B* from the *Black* series; 1 allele:
   B^+ full intense black

3. *C* from the *Cremello* series; 2 alleles:
   C^+ full colour
   C^{cr} dilutes full colour to cream

4. *D* from the *Dunning* series; 3 possible alleles:
   D^+ dilutes full colour to native dun
   D^D dilutes full colour to dun
   D^d has no influence

5. *E* from the *Extension* series; 2 alleles:
   E^+ full eumelanin production (all black)
   E^e switches eumelanin (black) production to phaeomelanin (all red) production

---

If we were to observe a grey horse without any knowledge of its background, we would not know whether its genotype was G^GG^G or G^GG^+. In this instance we record the unknown as a blank space underlined, $G^G\_$, to indicate the missing symbol could be either G^G or G^+.

BREEDING PREDICTIONS

Using simple genetic rules, a breeder can predict the traits that the offspring of a given mating can exhibit. The six possible ways in which a pair of genes can combine are illustrated in Figure 1.6. Ratios apply to expectancy over many matings, except in lines 1, 3 and 6 where exact expectancy is realised every time.

■ *Homozygous × like homozygous (line 1 & line 6)*
Let us breed two grey horses together. Obviously, $G^GG^G × G^GG^G$ produce only G^GG^G, i.e. grey horses. Similarly if we breed two non-greys together, $G^+G^+ × G^+G^+$, we produce only non-grey progeny.

> $G^GG^G × G^GG^G = G^GG^G$, or $G^+G^+ × G^+G^+ = G^+G^+$
> **RULE 1**

Rule 1. Homozygous bred to like homozygous always gives homozygous. The progeny will look like their parents and have the exact genotype of the parents (lines 1 and 6).

■ *Homozygous dominant × heterozygous dominant (line 2)*
Now, $G^GG^G × G^GG^+$ or $G^GG^+ × G^GG^G$ also gives a grey phenotype, but some progeny will be genotype G^GG^G and others will be G^GG^+.

> $G^GG^G × G^GG^+ = G^GG^G$ or G^GG^+
> **RULE 2**

Rule 2. Homozygous dominant bred to heterozygous dominant always gives both homozygous and heterozygous progeny, but these will always look like the parents (line 2).

■ *Homozygous dominant × homozygous recessive (line 3)*
What happens if we breed a pure-breeding grey to a non-grey? $G^GG^G × G^+G^+$ always gives G^GG^+. Grey is dominant over non-grey so 100 per cent will be grey.

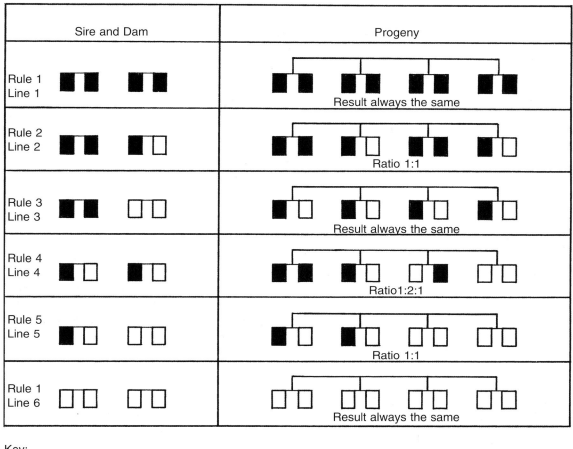

Key:

■ = dominant gene   □ = recessive gene

FIGURE 1.6 *Mendelian expectations*

Rule 3. When a homozygous dominant individual is bred to a recessive individual (which by its very definition is always homozygous), all progeny will look like the homozygous dominant parent, but unlike this parent they will be carriers (heterozygous) for the recessive gene (line 3).

■ *Heterozygous × heterozygous (line 4)*
What if we now breed progeny from the above mating together? The two heterozygous parents can only pass on to the progeny G^G or G^+ with equal chance of either being thrown (remember tossing a coin). The probabilities are 25 per cent $G^G G^G$, 50 per cent $G^G G^+$ and 25 per cent $G^+ G^+$. The first three genotypes have the same phenotype, so in reality 75 per cent will look grey, with 25 per cent being non-grey.

GREY sire × NON-GREY dam RULE 3

Parent genotype: $G^G G^G \times G^+ G^+$

Reproductive cells contain only G^G in the case of the sire, and only G^+ in the case of the mare.

G^G or G^G G^+ or G^+

Progeny
genotype: $G^G G^+$ $G^G G^+$ $G^G G^+$ $G^G G^+$

Probabilities: 25%   25%   25%   25%

Phenotype: Grey   Grey   Grey   Grey

13

Rule 4. When two heterozygotes are bred together the expected ratio of the progeny is 50 per cent the same as the parents, 25 per cent homozygous for the dominant gene, and 25 per cent homozygous for the recessive gene. This means 75 per cent will share the phenotype of the parents, and 25 per cent will be different in appearance (line 4).

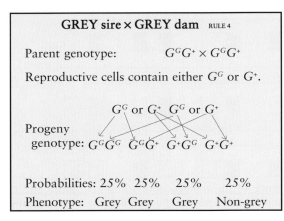

GREY sire × GREY dam RULE 4

Parent genotype: $G^GG^+ \times G^GG^+$

Reproductive cells contain either G^G or G^+.

Progeny
genotype: G^GG^G G^GG^+ G^+G^G G^+G^+

Probabilities: 25%   25%   25%   25%
Phenotype: Grey   Grey   Grey   Non-grey

■ *Heterozygous × recessive (line 5)*
We come to the final type of mating, a grey heterozygous parent bred to a non-grey. The probabilities are 50 per cent G^GG^+ and 50 per cent G^+G^+, which is 50 per cent grey and 50 per cent non-grey.

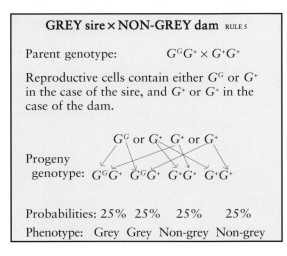

GREY sire × NON-GREY dam RULE 5

Parent genotype: $G^GG^+ \times G^+G^+$

Reproductive cells contain either G^G or G^+ in the case of the sire, and G^+ or G^+ in the case of the dam.

Progeny
genotype: G^GG^+ G^GG^+ G^+G^+ G^+G^+

Probabilities: 25%   25%   25%   25%
Phenotype: Grey   Grey   Non-grey   Non-grey

Rule 5. A heterozygous parent bred to a recessive parent will produce progeny like each parent in the ratio of 50 per cent each (line 5).

MULTIPLE COMBINATIONS

For very simple examples involving only one locus, the above method of calculating probabilities and ratios works very well. However, with colour breeding, we are frequently talking about several series at once (see Table B in Appendix, page 135). This is where it becomes more useful to use the so-called 'punnet square'. When crossing alleles from one series, for example, A, we have a simple cross (Table 1.1 below). If we use alleles from two series, for example, A and E, we have a dihybrid cross (Table 1.2 below); and if we use alleles from three series, for example, A, D and E, we have a trihybrid cross (see Table B in Appendix, page 134). The tables are examples of using punnet squares for calculations. For convenience, the symbols may be abbreviated.

Table 1.1   Heterozygous cross—A^AA^a sire × A^AA^a dam

sire	A or a	
dam		
A or a	AA	Aa
	aA	aa

Result: four combinations; ratio of offspring 1:2:1 or 25% AA, 50% Aa and 25% aa.

Table 1.2   Dihybrid cross—$A^AA^aE^+E^e$ sire × $A^AA^aE^+E^e$ dam

sire	AE	Ae	aE	ae
dam				
AE	$AAEE$	$AAEe$	$AaEE$	$AaEe$
Ae	$AAEe$	$Aaee$	$AaEe$	$Aaee$
aE	$AaEe$	$AaEe$	$aaEE$	$aaEe$
ae	$AaEe$	$Aaee$	$aaEe$	$aaee$

Result: sixteen combinations; ratio of offspring 9:3:3:1 or 56.25% AE, 18.75% $aaE\_$, 18.75% A_e, and 6.25% $aaee$.

ELIMINATING INFERIOR OR UNDESIRABLE GENES

If an undesirable gene, say parrot mouth, is dominant, it shows up in every generation; once the defect is removed from the breeding pool, that gene is eliminated. How many horses we cull is a matter of judgment but the choice is fairly clear.

Recessives are different. Individuals which are recessive (A^aA^a) could in some cases be inferior, that is, exhibit a weakness which should be culled, say cow hocks. If they are A^AA^a they could be normal. So long as they are not mated with another individual with A^a, the offspring will also appear normal. Close relations of the A^AA^a individual are more likely to have A^a (cow hocks) than matings at random. This is the danger of inbreeding—the latent weaknesses may be expressed. On the plus side, inbreeding reduces the ratio of heterozygotes and increases homozygosity (see rule 4, page 14), thus exposing weaknesses which may be culled and building on strengths. Most professional breeders will build a foundation of inbred stock to develop superior individuals, while removing those that prove to be inferior. The level of culling should increase with the degree of inbreeding used. Inbreeding is a most valuable tool that, wisely used, contributes greatly to overall breed improvement.

Recessive lethals
A lethal defect, which may or may not be caused by inherited factors, is one that causes death of the horse. An example of this is Combined Immuno-Deficiency (CID), a disease like AIDS in Arabian horses.

A recessive defect can be hidden by heterozygosity and, in practice, it is impossible to eliminate it completely. Even if a recessive is lethal, and most lethals are recessive, the carrier population can be quite substantial and in most cases the carrier cannot be detected. Frequently the carrier has a considerable selective advantage over the homozygote and this produces an equilibrium with the recessive lethal. In the case of Arabians that are carriers for CID, some breeders consider them to have more stamina and presence, thus the heterozygote is unknowingly favoured. With random matings in a very high population of 25 per cent carriers (according to a genetic principle known as the Hardy-Weinburg Law, a discussion

of which is outside the scope of this book), there is one chance in 64 of producing a recessive. With 10 per cent carriers the ratio is one in 400, and for 1 per cent carriers the ratio is one in 40 000.

These figures indicate the difficulty encountered if one wants to eliminate recessives and also highlights the fact that while there are many deleterious recessive alleles in a population, only a few are expressed.

Other lethal effects
In other species, many lethal effects that terminate early embryonic development are caused by chromosome aberrations. This is also likely to be the case in horses.

Partial and delayed effects
Many genes are not expressed at birth and can remain dormant before being exposed when the horse is mature, or even after it has passed breeding age. Examples in the horse are 'greying', and the occurrence of melanoma, which has a variable effect, sometimes resulting in death, in certain lines of grey horses. True lethals will kill the horse prior to, or shortly after, birth. Delayed lethals such as heart defects may not be expressed until later in life, or defects may be partial lethals which become lethal only under certain circumstances. An example of this is HYPP, a dominant delayed lethal somewhat similar to tying-up syndrome, which is present in some descendants of the Impressive line of Quarter Horses. Because the effect of this gene is delayed and only causes death in a small percentage of horses, it is very difficult to identify by observation (phenotype) alone.

Fortunately, a blood test has been developed which identifies HYPP individuals accurately, and horses testing HYPP positive may have their registration certificates stamped. Breeders can then decide to buy breeding stock in the knowledge that the defect can be bred out, while still maintaining the desirable bloodline in pedigrees. A horse that tests negative is proven to not possess the dominant gene, and it can be used for breeding in the knowledge that it is incapable of passing on HYPP.

SEX INFLUENCE

When the same combinations of genes express themselves differently in each sex, the phenotype is said to be sex influenced. This phenomenon will be more fully explained in Chapter 21, Spotted Horses.

LINKAGE

Two genes which exist at different loci on the same chromosome may be physically linked; when there is linkage, a foal will receive these same two genes from the parent animal at conception or none at all. The only way the two genes can dissociate is by a phenomenon known as crossing over (Figure 1.7). Because there are only 32 pairs of chromosomes and many thousands of genes on a chromosome, unless crossing over occurred, groups of genes would always be inherited together. Since crossing over occurs quite regularly, new combinations are created, and linkage is not so usual. Linkage has received little attention in horse colour studies, but it is known to occur in Paint Horse breeding. In some draft breeds, bay and roan appear to be linked. This means that more often when you get roan it will be bay, and when you get chestnut, it is less likely to be roan.

Sex linkage

Where linkage involves the X chromosome, genetic material is passed only from sire to daughter and from daughter to son or daughter. Heart size in the racehorse has been well researched as an example of X linkage inheritance. A son of a large heart size stallion can never inherit large heart size from his sire since he will only receive the X chromosome from his dam. Daughters may receive the gene for large heart size in single or double dose, depending on whether they had one or both parents with large heart size. Small 'fox ears' and wide forehead may also be X-linked.

Founder effect

'Founder effect' can confuse linkage studies. This refers to a set of alleles being established in a population through a relatively small number of foundation individuals. Some breeds even trace back to a single foundation animal. This may be due to breeding selection, or to geographical separation from a large genetic pool, such as occurs in small island populations. Certain characteristics can be inherited as a side-effect of a gene, which may

make these characteristics appear to be linked. These are known as *pleiotropic* effects; an example of this is the 'rat's tail' of the spotted coat pattern.

INTERMEDIATE EFFECTS

All-or-none differences are shown by traits inherited by simple dominant/recessive interactions, that is, tall peas crossed with short peas produces tall or short peas. It is as though a switch has been flicked to indicate presence or absence of a certain trait. More recently in genetics, other means of gene interaction besides the classic Mendelian principles have been discovered. The most simple of these, observed in colour breeding in horses, is the effect of *incomplete* or *partial dominance*.

This occurs when a heterozygous pair of genes has an equal or shared influence resulting in a phenotype intermediate between the two. It is like mixing paint, where red mixed with white gives pink. The ingredients are red and white but the result is pink. Incomplete dominance will be understood more readily when we discuss buckskin and palomino breeding. However, it is important to realise there is no pink gene, only red and white equivalents.

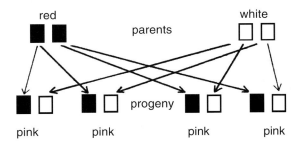

FIGURE 1.8 *Incomplete dominance. In this example, the progeny may be 'pink' but they can only pass on red or white genes*

MULTIFACTORIAL INHERITANCE

When we find full brothers and sisters with a range of expression of a single trait, we can assume additive (multifactorial) inheritance. Particular genes, known as *modifying* genes, have only a minor effect, but when large numbers of these are present the effect is cumulative. An example in the horse is the great range of variation in the presence and extent of white markings that may be observed in a certain family or bloodline.

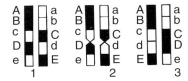

FIGURE 1.7 *Crossing over*

HOW IS COLOUR PRODUCED?

Coat colour is affected by pigment in the hair. There are two types of pigment in horse hair, eumelanin (you-mel-a-nin), a black pigment, and phaeomelanin (fee-o-mel-a-nin), a yellow-red pigment. These are both forms of melanin which is skin pigment. Melanin comes from specialised cells called melanocytes, of which there are two types, one containing skin pigment, the other without. Where there is no skin pigment, white hairs will be produced. Most horses have both types, which can sometimes switch. When a horse receives a deep skin injury, damaging the melanocytes, white scar hairs may grow back.

Factors which affect coat colour include melanin granule size, shape, number and arrangement in the hair (denser arrangement lightens hair), hair texture and structure, and intracellular environment.

In the horse coat colour is controlled by genes that:

- Produce black or red pigment in the hairs;
- Convert black or red to cream; or
- Do not produce pigment at all, creating white hairs.

Until recently, most of what we knew about colour inheritance came from studying other species, for example rats. Because they have similar sets of alleles, it is common for the same locus to cause an identical colour in horses. In the last few years coordinated international effort has made great progress towards mapping the genes responsible for certain disorders and those for hair colouring. Some information may help us understand similar conditions in humans or allow us to explain the mystery of apparent exceptions to current genetic understanding.

TRUE EXCEPTIONS FROM EXPECTED GENOTYPES

It is possible that true exceptions to the above rules of inheritance will occur as a result of factors currently unknown. These should be verified by parentage tests. All enlightened breed societies now insist on identification of breeding stock by parentage testing. There are two types of tests:

Bloodtyping: A blood sample is taken for testing in a recognised laboratory, which is matched with a sample from the sire and dam. Based on known inheritance of blood proteins, analysts are able to say whether the stated parentage is possible or impossible.

DNA testing: Similar to bloodtyping, except a hair sample is all that is required. The test measures genetic markers found in all DNA, and is cheaper and more accurate than bloodtyping. It is important that breed associations use only approved veterinary inspectors for such testing, to guard against malpractice.

Most exceptions prove to be the result of human error. The three most common errors are:

- Error in description of the foal or one of the parents.
- The stated sire was not, in fact, the genuine sire (another stallion stood on the property or a colt 'got in').
- The stated mare was not, in fact, the genuine dam. This happens usually when two mares foal at roughly the same time and the foals inadvertently swap dams, unknown to the owner. I have even heard of this to have happened when foals crossed through a fence.

In other species exceptions are thought to be the result of extremely rare genes that suppress the appearance of another, or mechanisms not yet reported in horses. Of course there is always the possibility, though rare, of mutation. Mutations in coat colour patterns were often kept and prized.

This allowed the mutation to spread through the horse population. Such horses survived as they were protected from predators. Most mutations have minor effects and could pass unnoticed for several generations. Other mutants prove to be abnormal in some way.

Exceptions prove that we do not know everything there is to know about breeding, but it is important to realise that because the unexplained can sometimes occur, though rarely, we cannot plan for it. Breeding programs must be planned around known information and that is what this book is all about.

PART 2

BASE COLOURS

We now move on to investigate the genetic background of our horse's colour. The whole force of this part of the book is that there are only the two pigment colours in the horse, black and red, and their presence, alteration or absence determines coat colour.

Australian Stock Horse lineup

2

CHESTNUT

Quick Guide: Chestnut

- Chestnut is a red horse of any shade.
- There are six main shades based on the combination of genes for dark, medium or light red, with sootiness or its absence.
- All shades of chestnut may have a flaxen mane or tail.
- Chestnut is the most recessive colour.
- Non-chestnut parents may have chestnut foals.
- Chestnut bred to chestnut always gives chestnut.

Although described as 'red', chestnut can be very dark as in liver, or very light as in 'blonde' or sorrel. The legs, mane and tail are also reddish.

Standard chestnut Australian Stock Horse stallion Rannock, owned by the author

The chestnut has red granules in its hair, as a result of E^e (from the *Extension* series) which is recessive and therefore chestnut can only exist as a homozygote, that is, as E^eE^e. This is the reason why chestnut bred to chestnut must always produce chestnut (rule 1, line 6, page 12).

Since the realisation of this law of genetics by various stud book societies, recognition has not been given to any other colours born from chestnut parents. The only exceptions to this rule have been very rare white foals. This is explained by the 'sabino-white' factor discussed in a later chapter, where we will learn that these are not really exceptions at all.

The variation in the shades of chestnut are the result of genes of the *F* series (for *Flaxen*), and other series, which give brown (tan), red and yellow shades. These roughly equate to dark, medium and light. The boundaries between these shades are never clear-cut so there is much overlap. Attempts to categorise the different shades of chestnut into genotype has, to date, been unsuccessful, making breeding predictions as to the type of chestnut that will result from a mating difficult.

The most commonly observed chestnut is the standard chestnut, a carroty-orange colour, but

Action of the *Agouti* series on chestnut

$A^+\_E^eE^e$	Light chestnut
$A^A\_E^eE^e$	Red chestnut
$A^t\_E^eE^e$	Standard chestnut
$A^aA^aE^eE^e$	Liver chestnut

Footnote to table

Allele *A*, from the *Agouti* series, influences eumelanin pigment: alleles from this series are thought to influence the shade of chestnut.

Allele *E*, from the *Extension* series, influences phaeomelanin production: E^e causes phaeomelanin production, which results in chestnut.

LEFT TO RIGHT: *Shoulders of red, standard and 'false' liver chestnuts*

mud-brown, bronze, copper, red, red-purple, liver, chocolate and almost black are observed. Light colours include golden, sandy and 'blonde', the palest shade of chestnut.

The Western breeds use the term 'sorrel' to describe these light shades, with 'chestnut' used only for red, mud-brown or liver. However, I prefer to call them all chestnut as attempts to categorise them into different shades are often misleading, especially when, due to seasonal changes, a mud chestnut may appear liver, or a golden chestnut becomes red.

Chestnut may be altered by the modifying gene *Sty*, which causes sootiness, an admixture of black/liver-brown hairs throughout, including the tail. Due to seasonal conditions these can appear as dapples or change the horse to a 'false' liver.

Some breeders also describe the chestnut with dark mane and tail. It has been my experience that these horses will colour up in the body to match the darker shade of the mane and tail, given certain nutritional and environmental conditions. Chestnut is the easiest colour to breed because one only needs chestnut parents. If a non-chestnut parent produces a chestnut foal, no matter what colour its mate, it is proof that the non-chestnut parent carries the chestnut gene E^e.

If a chestnut foal is bred from non-chestnut parents that have no known chestnuts in their immediate pedigree it is proof that both parents, no matter how unlikely, carry the chestnut gene E^e.

Light chestnut crossed together will give all shades of sorrel and chestnut, unless homozygous, but the darker chestnuts will give only dark chestnut. There has been some debate among geneticists as to whether true liver is part of the chestnut family, or whether it is a separate colour in its own right. Most accept that it is not a separate colour.

Honey chestnut (sorrel) Haflinger with white mane and tail (photo J. Hele)

Sandy chestnut (sorrel) with ivory points, and mismark on flank, Welsh pony Hazelmere Colleen

when the body itself fades. All shades of chestnut may have a light mane and tail if $F^f F^f$ is present. In most cases $F^f F^f$ also causes lighter lower legs; $F^f F^f$ may even inhibit the presence of smut marks (discussed in Chapter 22). Frequently, the mane is lighter than the tail, or vice versa. In many horses, the light mane and tail grows out completely to ordinary chestnut by the time the horse is four or five and it is uncertain whether these horses are $F^f F^f$, or an aberration of normal chestnut F^F_.

Obviously the flaxen mane and tail can only be expressed if the horse is chestnut, because by definition a bay, brown or black will have a black mane and tail. Black, brown and bay horses can be $F^f F^f$ in their genotype. Very rarely (nearly always in the Arabian breed), gene F^f 'penetrates' even in a bay horse and silver-streaked tails (known as 'silver-tails') are observed. Light manes and tails are highly regarded in the Arabian, Belgian, Jutland, Suffolk Punch, Welsh and the Haflinger, the last of which is almost exclusively this colour. It is an ideal colour for palomino breeding because of the absence of black hairs.

Some horsemen attribute soft skin and a highly strung nature to the chestnut, in much the same way that redheads in people are thought to be 'fiery'. I have observed hundreds of chestnuts and never found a trend of any significance. Temperament is very much an individual trait.

However, it is true that the occurrence of white markings in chestnut horses is likely to be more extensive than the white markings in horses of other colours. This is useful knowledge when selecting foundation stock for pinto breeding.

Among the horse breeds of the world there are some which are exclusively chestnut, including the Haflinger pony, the Suffolk Punch and Schleswig; and some which are predominantly chestnut, such as the Belgian and Morgan. (Draught horse lore refers to these as 'chesnut'.) In addition, the King Ranch Quarter Horse was mostly liver chestnut due to inbreeding to the liver stallion The Ol' Sorrel.

FLAXEN CHESTNUT

An appealing colour seen in many breeds is the chestnut with light mane and tail, known as flaxen. The mane may be honey-coloured, 'grey' (light with black hairs), flaxen, ivory or, rarely, white. The gene responsible is F^f, and normal horses are F^+. Under certain seasonal conditions, F^+ may make the mane and tail appear darker than the rest of the body,

POINTS OF THE CHESTNUT

The mane, tail, and lower legs of horses are referred to as the 'points'. The Spanish terms are sometimes used for three types of point colour in chestnuts: *alazan* (red points), *ruano* (points lighter than the body or flaxen) and *tostado* (brown points). In breeds where chestnut is the predominant colour, the Spanish descriptions are useful identifiers. However, these assume that point colour is the same for mane and tail, as well as the legs, which is not always the case, and that colour does not alter seasonally. For these reasons, the terms are not used in this book.

3

BLACK

Quick Guide: Black

- A black horse is all black, except that white markings may be present.
- Black is the second most recessive colour after chestnut (red).
- The E series controls black ($E^+\_$) and red (E^eE^e).
- Black bred to black gives black or chestnut.
- Homozygous black (E^+E^+) can never produce a chestnut foal.
- There are two types of black horse, fading and non-fading.
- The goal of black breeders is the jet black.
- Non-fading black (jet black) is recessive to fading black due to the intensifying gene being affected by the fading gene.
- Fading black bred to fading black can give jet black.
- Jet black bred to jet black gives jet black in 75 per cent of progeny and dark chestnut in 25 per cent.

The genuinely black-coloured horse is particularly striking, especially in combination with white markings such as a star or socks. A true black has a black body colour, as well as black in all the soft parts, whether or not it has white markings (which are irrelevant to the definition). The presence of brown or lighter coloured hairs on the muzzle, eyebrows, flanks or inner areas of the breast disqualifies the horse from being black. Horse breeders describe two types of black horse: non-fading and fading black.

Two black Australian Stock Horse stallions, Rivoli Ray (left) and Proud Boy (right); Proud Boy proved to be homozygous. The same horse can look either of the two colours photographed, depending on reflected light, and it may be very difficult to separate the fading black from non-fading black without a history of the horse

NON-FADING BLACK

Also known as raven or jet black, this is born charcoal or blue-black (or, rarely, black already), changes to jet black and fades, if at all, only under extreme conditions. In good condition it has a metallic, iridescent or bluish shine.

FADING BLACK

Usually born smoky/ashen-coloured but may be born dark bay or brown. As an adult, it fades to a minor or greater degree, and usually needs a rug or stable to bring out its best colour. The shine on the horse is rarely metallic in sunlight.

Fading to a reddish-brown is a common occurrence in blacks that are exposed to the weather. The hairs typically sunburn on the ends of the mane and throughout the coat. Black will also burn from sweat, the most common areas here being around the girth, neck and brow. This type of horse is still a black.

Some colours commonly mistaken for black are:

- **Dilute black** This is actually the darkest form of buckskin, and may be so dark as to be indistinguishable from true black in some instances. Dilute black is born a yellowish or pumpkin colour, becomes smoky black in good coat and almost always fades to a dusty black or rusty liver colour when out of coat.
- **Brown** The English term is black-brown, the American seal-brown. It describes the darkest form of brown. It may have a jet black body but the lighter muzzle and flanks are the giveaway. The muzzle colouring is usually more obvious in winter coat.

Black is formed as a result of a switch in the *Extension* series to the allele E^+, so black horses are E^+E^+ or E^+E^e. Locus B produces black pigmentation (*eumelanin*), which is unaffected by E^+, so the horse remains black. For chestnut, E^eE^e interacts epistatically with locus B to convert eumelanin to phaeomelanin (red). Although the genes which cause fading in the black horse have not been identified, it is likely its presence is dominant over its absence. Jet black is the most intensive colour of all.

Black is easily bred, being, in effect, the second most recessive colour after chestnut. Two blacks bred together can produce only black or chestnut (rule 4, line 4, page 13). I have known of several homozygous black stallions and naturally these have never produced a chestnut foal. A homozygous black sire will produce bay, brown or black to chestnut mares; the reason for this will be explained in Chapter 5.

Whilst it is striking, black is a colour not frequently selected by horsemen aiming to use horses in harsh terrain, such as the Australian outback. The colour absorbs heat too readily and the hide becomes more sensitive than that of other horses with dark skin. Certainly the countries where black horses have been selectively bred are those with the colder climates—Ariège Pony, Canadian Horse, Fell, Friesian Draught, Percheron and Shetland Pony.

4

BAY AND BROWN

Quick Guide: Bay and Brown

- Brown is a black horse that has been genetically altered to have lighter colour in the soft parts.
- Bay is a black horse that has been genetically altered to have a lighter, mostly red body colour and head, leaving black in the legs, mane and tail.
- The genetic alteration is brought about by genes of the *A* series, which result in bay being dominant over brown, and brown is dominant over black.

Black is generally regarded as under the control of the *B* locus which produces black pigmentation in all species. Hair colour is then determined by other genes which alter the amount, accumulation and distribution of the pigment in the hair cortex, which in horses produces bay, brown or other colours.

BAY

Bay is defined as a red-brown body colour with black legs, mane and tail. Frequently the ears are tipped with black. A dorsal stripe, if present, is black. Bay can sometimes have a cast of black through the coat, caused by the intermediate effects of A^a and A^t, or the *Sooty* factor (at the *Sty*

Blood bay Quarter Horse stallion Jet Master (imp.USA).

locus), described in Chapter 22.

Shades commonly described by horsemen are:

- **Standard bay** Plain red body without an admixture of darker or lighter hairs.
- **Blood bay** A dark blood-red, almost purple shade throughout.
- **Mahogany bay** Brown-red, with the coat showing some variation of dark and light shades throughout.
- **Copper bay** Orange-red throughout.
- **Golden bay** The golden bay has limited red and looks yellowish, still with black points.
- **Light bay** The light bay is not to be confused with the lightest shades of bay above. It refers to the bay without strongly marked points, the domestic equivalent of the original wild bay. Frequently the mane is 'off-black' and black on the legs appears only on the fetlocks.

It is interesting that although bay is one of the most universally prized colours, being exceptionally hardy in all climates and terrains, only one breed has been developed around the colour, the Cleveland Bay.

BROWN

Shades of brown or black hair are spread over the body except in the soft parts, those areas around the muzzle, eyebrows, quarters, flank and girth which show a gradation to lighter colour. These areas are quite frequently described as 'mealy' if

ABOVE: *Standard bay Australian Stock Horse Chalani Wildstar*
LEFT: *Flank of mahogany bay*
BELOW: *Mahogany bays, breed unknown*

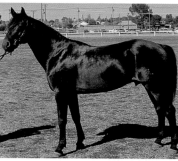

ABOVE: *Master Herbert (sire Rannock)*
LEFT: *Little Abbey — both are seal-brown Australian Stock Horse stallions*

yellowish, but may be red or liver-brown. Rarely, the mane may be liver instead of black due to fading. The darkest copper-nosed brown, or 'black and tan' as it is sometimes known in Europe, is called 'seal-brown' in the United States.

Brown is not even considered a separate colour in some registries, or by some researchers, merely a shade of bay. It is useful to treat brown as a colour on its own, however, because most practical horsemen do so. In this book, brown is considered in its own right, and includes seal-brown, as well as light brown.

The Canadian Horse is a breed that is exclusively brown or black. Developed in the French-speaking areas from original foundation stock, it has acquired an excellent reputation for versatility and hardiness.

ABOVE: *Standard brown Quarter Horse Chalani Paper Tiger*
RIGHT: *The near-black Australian Stock Horse Chalani Giselle must be classed as brown because of brown on the nose (sire Master Herbert)*

25

5

INTERRELATIONSHIPS BETWEEN BASE COLOURS

Quick Guide: Base Colours

- The base colours are black, brown, bay and chestnut.
- In general, lighter colours are dominant over darker colours.
- The A series in combination with E^+ produces bay, brown and black.
- The A series in combination with E^e controls the various shades of chestnut, although often we can't tell by looking at a chestnut horse which A gene is present.
- Chestnut bred to black can produce black, brown or bay, depending on which shade of chestnut is used, as well as chestnut.
- Liver chestnut may be used to produce jet black, when the other parent is black.
- Breeds of bay, brown or black still produce the occasional chestnut, even after many generations of selective breeding.
- All horses are homozygous for the B locus which gives black pigment.
- For convenience then, B locus is left out of calculations.

All horses are homozygous for the B locus which gives black pigment, that is B^+B^+. This is altered in horses that are not black by genes at other loci, especially the A and E series. The first alteration is produced by the allele A^t which changes the soft parts to lighter red or yellow, but keeps the black coat over the body, thus creating a brown horse. The second alteration, brought about by the A^A allele, restricts the black pigment to the legs, mane, tail and ear tips. The horse will be bay. There is yet another allele, A^+, which creates the light bay. The most recessive allele, A^a, has no effect at all, so as A^aA^a the horse remains black. If it is understood that, very loosely speaking, lighter colours are more dominant than darker ones, we can arrive at the scale shown opposite.

How does one interpret the chart? Usually, a stallion bred to a mare of the same colour can produce only foals of the same colour or a colour lower down on the list, that is, bay × bay can produce bay, brown or black, but brown × brown can produce only brown or black.

The A series is known as the *Agouti* or wild series and many A alleles have been found in other species.

Action of the *Agouti* series on *Black*

$A^+\_\ B^+B^+$	light bay	Greatest dominance
$A^A\_\ B^+B^+$	bay	
$A^t\_\ B^+B^+$	brown	
$A^aA^aB^+B^+$	black	Most recessive

Footnote to table

As all horses are B^+B^+, for convenience in calculations this is left out of all further charts and understood as present.

In horses, the wild or ancestral colour is the red sandy bay/dun with pale belly and primitive marks, now seen only in the Przewalski's horse. Rare crosses of Przewalski's horse with the domestic horse have produced progeny of an intermediate colour.

The ancestral gene may have mutated to the dun seen in Fjord ponies, the mouse-bay seen in the Exmoor pony, the golden Akhal-Teke, and the dun of the now extinct Tarpan.

The A series is used to designate the various shades of bay and brown. The alleles probably have intermediate effects so that the distinctions between the colours are not clear-cut. This series cannot be viewed in isolation, only in conjunction with the E (*Extension*) series. The A series controls the distribution of pigment. In the presence of E^+, all horses will have black pigment either totally, as in the true black, or partially, as in the brown or bay. Red conversion, E^e, creates the chestnut and sorrel. It is also possible that $A^A A^A$ horses are redder than $A^A A^a$ horses, as the experience of some palomino breeders would suggest.

Genotypes of the base colours

Progeny calculations are made by using a dihybrid cross (see Chapter 1, page 14).

$A^+\_ \ E^+\_$	Light bay	$A^+\_ \ E^e E^e$	Light chestnut
$A^A\_ \ E^+\_$	Bay	$A^A\_ \ E^e E^e$	Red chestnut
$A^t\_ \ E^+\_$	Brown	$A^t\_ \ E^e E^e$	Standard chestnut
$A^a A^a \ E^+\_$	Black	$A^a A^a E^e E^e$	Liver chestnut

The darker chestnut colours bred together can only produce the darker chestnuts, but as with breeding for bay, identifying the particular shade of chestnut is not always easy. Two other factors, *Sooty* (*Sty* locus) and *Flaxen* (*F* locus), serve to complicate the issue. The sooty chestnuts are particularly sensitive to fading and may look chestnut with dark mane and tail sometimes, and dappled liver at other times. Because of environmental factors, the chestnut shade is not a reliable indicator of A locus makeup. Unfortunately, although most breeding programs fit the above chart very neatly, there is still a lot to be learnt about the interrelationship of black, brown and bay, particularly as the boundaries between the colours are not clear-cut and identification is difficult.

There is still disagreement amongst geneticists about the inheritance of bay and brown. Some consider brown to be dominant over bay. Personal experience does not support this. Many browns are foaled from two bay parents. The homozygous blood bay Quarter Horse stallion Jet Master (imp.USA), which I knew personally, sired well over 100 foals. Even though many of the mares he was bred to were browns, not one single brown foal resulted, which would have been impossible unless bay (A^A) was dominant over brown (A^t). The well-known Cleveland Bay, developed in England as a high-calibre carriage horse, is only ever registered as bay. Chestnuts do occur very rarely, illustrating that even after 400 years of pure and selective breeding, it is difficult to completely erase recessive characteristics. The solution is to cull both dam and sire (rule 4, line 4, page 13). Often only the dam is culled. As the stallion usually has the greater influence on a breed, this is a mistake.

With a Cleveland Bay stallion, test-breeding to five chestnut non-Cleveland mares would give a sound but not completely foolproof guide as to whether the stallion carried the chestnut gene—accuracy would be to 97 per cent. One chestnut foal would be enough to prove the stallion a carrier so that he could be avoided for pure-breeding purposes.

With a mare it is much more difficult to prove homozygosity as she is unlikely to have enough foals. One bay Australian Stock Horse mare we owned produced seven bay foals in a row to chestnut sires, but her eighth and last foal was a black, by one of the same stallions! It would have been easy to have assumed that she was homozygous for A^A if we had not put her in foal the eighth time! A DNA-based test for chestnut carrier parents, known as the Red Factor Test, is now available through the Veterinary Genetics Laboratory at the University of California (Davis campus).

If black colour is desired, one needs $A^a A^a$ in the genotype. This can be obtained by utilising liver chestnut as one of the parents. True liver is thought to be controlled by the same intensifying gene as jet black, so is the ideal choice for black production when two black parents are unavailable. This information is of use in breeds which do not have many black or brown horses, such as the Arabian. The Arabian breed in Australia, which has always had a number of liver chestnuts and many bays, rarely produced black or brown foals until the upsurge in black Arabian importation in the 1970s. Linkage of A^a to E^e seems the only plausible explanation, although some have suggested another allele, E^B or *Extension brown*, to explain this phenomenon. This suggestion is unlikely in view of the fact that, historically, the Arabian has had more influence on the world's breeds than any other, yet E^B, if it exists at all, is rare among those breeds.

The base colours of black, brown, bay and chestnut, together with grey, are referred to as the 'Thoroughbred' colours, for these are the only colours found in the Thoroughbred and its base breed, the Arabian. Most other light horse breeds in the world derive from these two. Numerically they are the largest group of purebreds in the world, so are ideal for crossbreeding experiments to prove colour rules, except where homozygosity for a non-Thoroughbred colour is required.

PART 3

DILUTE COLOURS

The four colours discussed so far are termed base colours. Any other colour is a modification of chestnut, black, bay or brown. The palomino, buckskin, taffy, dun and composites of these colours are, in fact, dilutions of the basic four coat colours. There are three main types of dilution mechanisms in the horse. They are the *Cremello* dilution, a form of partial albinism, the *Dunning* dilution, and the *Taffy* dilution.

Seasonal dark palomino Australian Stock Horse mare Chalani Tamara and foal

6

CREMELLO

Quick Guide: Dilution Mechanisms

- The three main types of dilution in horses; cremello, dun and taffy.
- In double dose, the cremello dilution produces the pseudo-albinos cremello, perlino and smoky perlino.
- Pseudo-albinos are to be avoided in breeding programs due to the limited economic value, and in some breeds are not granted recognition.
- Cremello dilution is incompletely dominant with base colours, giving an intermediate effect (e.g. palomino or buckskin).
- The eyes of a pseudo-albino are not pink.

THE CREMELLO DILUTION

The horse has only two recognised alleles of this series, C^+ representing full pigment manufacture of normal colours, and C^{cr} representing almost complete absence of pigment in homozygous form as evidenced by the pseudo-albinos (cremello and perlino). It is from the pseudo-albinos that the palominos and buckskins are produced. The hairs of C^{cr} horses have fewer and smaller pigment granules than do those of C^+C^+ individuals, and the granules tend to be concentrated toward the tips of the hairs, hence the diluted effect. In the horse C^+ is incompletely dominant to C^{cr}; in other words, full colour is incompletely dominant to cremello dilution. This can be summarised as follows:

Incomplete action of *Cremello* dilution series

$C^+ C^+$ = full colour (black, brown, bay or chestnut)
$C^+ C^{cr}$ = dilute colour (buckskin, palomino)
$C^{cr} C^{cr}$ = double dilute or pseudo-albino (perlino, cremello)

THE PSEUDO-ALBINO

It seems odd that true albinos are common in other species, including humans, but not one confirmed report exists for the horse. The true albino would have white hair with pink skin and eyes, the latter due to blood illuminated by light rays passing through the translucent tissue of the eye. This discrepancy between species suggests the cremello dilution is unlike albinism in mice or humans, or the partial albinism (Siamese, Himalayan, Burmese) of the cat. The locus for cremello dilution may be unique to the horse. In many countries the pseudo-albino coat is referred to as 'blue-eyed cream'. The body colour is typically off-white with just enough colouration to enable distinction to be made between the body colour and white markings such as stars, socks or even the broken colour of the pinto pseudo-albino. The underlying skin is pink; eyes are a pale glass-blue.

The pseudo-albino is the subject of much interest amongst horse people. Many believe, quite wrongly, that horses of this colour will be blind or deaf, although the eyesight of the pseudo-albino varies greatly from individual to individual.

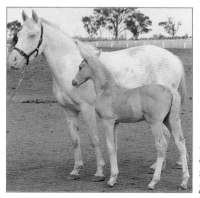

Cremello Australian Stock Horse mare with palomino foal

Compared with the normal brown or amber eye, the glass-blue eye is partially deficient of pigment and will absorb much more light than the eye can reasonably be expected to cope with. The cremello mare illustrated was particularly sensitive. Sunlight, heat and pressure may irritate the skin or even cause blisters and skin cancers. If allowed to weather naturally, some will suntan to a pumpkin colour which gives a little protection. Steady work often results in chafing. Is it any wonder then that Australian stockmen have avoided this colour more than any other? Nevertheless, in metropolitan areas and the cooler climates they do quite well, leading useful and productive lives.

The cremello and perlino

The two types of pseudo-albino are well documented in the literature. The most common is the cremello which has a white or ivory mane and tail, whilst the perlino is frequently associated with a darker coffee-coloured mane and tail. The distinction is not always so easy however, for most perlinos cannot be distinguished from cremellos by appearance. One Welsh stallion I knew was a proven perlino, yet the only hint of his being visually different from the cremello was a few coffee-coloured dapples apparent in spring as he changed into summer coat.

Smoky perlino This is the darkest shade of perlino, and has points which are yellowish, light sooty or smoky blue with smoky mane and tail. The genetic difference between perlino and cremello is a result of the presence of genes of the other base colours. If genes of the series A and E represent the basic colours bay, brown or black, the perlino is formed. If they represent chestnut, the cremello results. The cremello/perlino or double dilute is generally produced from the breeding of two single dilute individuals, such as buckskin to

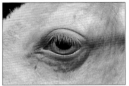

ABOVE: *Smoky perlino Welsh, both parents dilute black, and eye of same horse (photos J. Wiersema)*

The pseudo-albino		
$C^{cr}C^{cr} + \_\_E^eE^e$	(chestnut)	= cremello
$C^{cr}C^{cr} + A^A\_E^+E^+$	(bay)	= perlino
$C^{cr}C^{cr} + A^t\_E^+E^+$	(brown)	= perlino
$C^{cr}C^{cr} + A^aA^aE^+E^+$	(black)	= smoky perlino

buckskin or palomino to palomino, but sometimes grey may mask C^{cr}.

It is important to know the original colour of a grey before breeding it if a cremello/perlino is to be avoided.

This is particularly important in breeds which do not permit cremellos or perlinos to be registered, such as Quarter Horses and Morgans. Any grey that was born a dilute colour, such as palomino, before turning grey, is a candidate for producing the pseudo-albino.

Remember, no full-coloured horse (C^+C^+) can ever produce a pseudo-albino, regardless of whether it has a pseudo-albino ancestor, because its genotype does not contain the necessary C^{cr} allele for cremello or perlino production (rule 1, line 1, page 12). Certain breeds such as the Arabian, Thoroughbred, Haflinger and most draught breeds contain only the full colours in their gene pool. Others such as the Australian Pony, Australian Stock Horse, Icelandic Pony, Miniature Horse, Paso Fino, Peruvian Paso and other gaited breeds, and the Shetland, allow double dilutes. While horsemen may not appreciate the pseudo-albino from a performance viewpoint, many are now appreciating them for their breeding value. It is from the perlino and cremello that some of the horse's most attractive colours, the dilutes, may be produced.

Perlino Clark Kent, breed unknown

7

PALOMINO

Quick Guide: Palomino

- The ideal palomino is gold with white mane and tail.
- Genetic palomino is any shade of gold, sooty or cream, caused by the dilution of chestnut.
- There is no palomino gene therefore palomino can *never* become a breed.
- Palomino bred to palomino gives a 25 per cent of producing cremello.
- Palomino bred to palomino gives a 50 per cent chance of producing palomino.
- Palomino bred to chestnut *never* produces cremello.
- Palomino bred to chestnut gives a 50 per cent chance of producing palomino.
- Cremello bred to chestnut gives a 100 per cent chance of producing palomino.
- The ideal chestnut for palomino production is the cherry red with flaxen mane and tail.
- The parents should not exhibit smuts, spots, patches, dapples or white or dark hairs.

True-coloured palomino, part-Arabian, Brandwood Little Jim

The pseudo-albino or double dilute may be crossed with any base colour to produce a single dilute colour. The single dilutes are the family of palominos and buckskins, which range from pale cream to dark sooty and almost chocolate. The great range of variation is dependent upon the shade of base colour on which the dilute C^{cr} is acting, as the mechanism is that of incomplete dominance, not the classic Mendelian inheritance we have discussed previously.

$$C^+C^+ \text{ (chestnut)} \times C^{cr}C^{cr} \text{ (pseudo-albino)}$$
$$= C^+C^{cr} \text{ (palomino)}$$

Full colour is diluted to an intermediate colour. In the case of chestnuts, colour is diluted to the palomino, but the exact shade of palomino is determined by A and other series which regulate the shade of chestnut.

The most desirable colour for a registered Palomino is considered to be 'between three shades lighter or darker than a newly minted gold coin'. This colour was known in Australia as 'sovereign creamy' until the formation of Palomino Associations. Those of us fortunate enough to have seen a newly minted gold coin would be few indeed. A golden cigarette wrapper may be a more useful comparison. What constitutes a shade? Some may be surprised to learn that a gold coin is nowhere near as dark as most people's ideal of a golden palomino.

The situation is further confused by the fact that most palominos are seasonal. It is important to look at the horse in summer and in full adult coat. The best coloured palominos will be born more an apricot or pink colour rather than cream, and as adults will not demonstrate much appreciable coat colour change from winter to summer. However, many acceptable palominos vary considerably by changing from cream to golden in summer. Frequently, those considered a good colour in

Shades of chestnut and palomino

Light chestnut $(A^+\_)$ + dilution (C^{cr})
  = cream (or cream palomino)
Red chestnut $(A^A\_)$ + dilution (C^{cr})
  = golden palomino
Chestnut $(A^t\_)$ + dilution (C^{cr})
  = seasonal palomino
Liver chestnut (A^aA^a) + dilution (C^{cr})
  = chocolate (or sooty) palomino

winter change to too dark and sooty in summer. Occasionally, one will change to a colour difficult to distinguish from light chestnut or taffy. How dark is too dark?

BREEDING PALOMINOS

From a hereditary point of view, a palomino *must* carry the dilution gene, and will be a palomino no matter how dark it looks, provided it is paired with a chestnut gene. Very light golden Haflingers and

True-coloured palomino with much admired white markings, Waveney Lynton. Note also spots (smuts) on rump

Iridescence and gold shine in a true-coloured palomino with chestnut foal

Sooty palomino. Young horse already too dark and will darken further

Gold. Palomino-bred, mane and tail too dark. This colour is sometimes known as lemonsilla

A foal born this colour usually stays true-coloured

The cherry red chestnut shade ideal for palomino breeding (Barrister Farms Saddlebreds)

Thoroughbreds are sometimes mistakenly referred to as palominos. These cannot be regarded as palominos because no cremello dilution (C^{cr}) exists in these breeds. (If it did cremello would also occur.) When the horse in question is of unknown breeding, identification is far less certain, and it may only be possible to decide after it has had a single dilute foal to a base-coloured mate.

One guide used by palomino breeders is that a chestnut, no matter how light, will always shine red or copper, while a palomino, no matter how dark, will always shine gold or silver. This proves to be fairly accurate. When breeding, it is important to consider the amount of problem hairs. Are there too many hairs that are not a clear gold, with the horse's coat including dark hairs, black hairs or white hairs?

It is important to start with breeding stock which do not exhibit these problems if ideal colour is desired, for although good colour is produced in some instances, this is not at all reliable. Avoid roans and greys, pintos and Appaloosas.

Which is the best colour chestnut to use when breeding palominos?

The $A^A A^A$ flaxen chestnut is ideal for crossbreeding, because this is the richest red colour, and dilutes to true gold. Palominos from this cross exhibit the least seasonal variation. The dilution gene C^{cr} is ineffective on black hairs, so choose a chestnut free of smuts, spots and dapples. The only insurance against dark hairs in the mane and tail is to use chestnuts with flaxen manes/tails. When a good coloured chestnut cannot be found, make certain the palomino used is a good colour. Rich blood bay ($A^A A^A$) can also produce good coloured palominos, provided the bay is known to be a chestnut carrier ($E^+ E^e$).

The reason some palomino breeders experience difficulty breeding good coloured palominos from chestnuts is because they do not use the right coloured base chestnut. Palomino breeders have tended to use the more readily available standard chestnut instead of the cherry red. This produces too many dark hairs in the mane and tail, or body. The results have been seasonal palominos which are usually white or cream in winter and gold or sooty in summer. Using bright red chestnut overcomes this difficulty while using flaxen chestnut tends to give the preferred white mane and tail.

Some breeders like to use two palomino parents rather than the accepted palomino/chestnut cross. This is because they can evaluate the correct colour of both parents. Crosses made in this manner produce excellent colour but run the risk of producing a cremello ($C^{cr} C^{cr}$), where no risk of producing cremello occurs with the recommended palomino/chestnut cross. Because the palomino is a result of incomplete dominance, the result of a single dilution crossed with a chestnut, there is no such thing as a pure-bred palomino. Many generations of crossing palomino to palomino can never result in the production of a homozygous or pure-breeding palomino. Indeed, the illustrations in this chapter serve to show that the probability of producing palomino from palomino crosses is identical to the probability of producing palomino from palomino/chestnut crosses.

I believe that the only way to breed top quality horses is to use at least one pure-bred parent. In the nineteenth century it was the Arab, in the twentieth century the Thoroughbred, that was on top for breed improvement. It is a statistical fact that the best performance horses in the world are carrying top Thoroughbred blood. Breeders who are serious about quality and performance will cross with a top quality purebred such as the Thoroughbred, to take advantage of what the purebred has to offer their palomino breeding programs. This means palomino × chestnut is the breeding combination of choice.

Why not use a cremello to cross with a chestnut and thus produce palomino 100 per cent of the time? (rule 3, line 3, page 13).

Why not indeed! This is the most logical approach, and could probably put some palomino stallion owners out of business.

No doubt it is the only reason why all except enlightened palomino groups throughout the world have decided that this cross is taboo. These fears are probably quite groundless, however, because of the extreme difficulty in finding a good quality cremello stallion which also has the ideal base chestnut genotype for palomino production. The parents of any such cremello stallion must be true gold palominos.

It must be remembered that seasonal palominos are subject to the influence of nutrition and hormones. Stallions and geldings have a more even hormone balance, so hardest of all is to produce a true golden mare which retains her colour irrespective of season or food. Some palominos are not even the same colour from one year to the next!

Iridescence

Many palominos carry an almost luminous metallic sheen known as iridescence. The finer the coat the more likely it is that iridescence will be evident. This is often also seen in chestnuts and buckskins, seldom in duns. Iridescence is under nutritional, hormonal and genetic control. The Akhal-Teke, an ancient breed of horse from Turkmenistan, is almost exclusively iridescent.

Popular crosses for producing palomino

Palomino bred to palomino (rule 4, line 4, page 13):
$C^+ C^{cr} \times C^+ C^{cr} = C^+ C^+$ chestnut (25%), $C^+ C^{cr}$ palomino (50%) and $C^{cr} C^{cr}$ cremello (25%)

Palomino bred to chestnut (rule 5, line 5, page 13):
$C^+ C^{cr} \times C^+ C^+ = C^+ C^+$ chestnut (50%) and $C^+ C^{cr}$ palomino (50%)

Chestnut bred to cremello (rule 3, line 3, page 13):
$C^+ C^+ \times C^{cr} C^{cr} = C^+ C^{cr}$ cremello (100%)

8

BUCKSKIN

Quick Guide: Buckskin

- The cremello dilution acting on bay, brown or black produces a genetic buckskin, which may be cream, yellow, gold, sooty or off-black.
- Golden buckskin, long regarded as favourite, is a coppery gold body with black legs, mane and tail.
- There is no buckskin gene so buckskin can never become a breed.
- Buckskin bred to buckskin gives a one in four chance of producing the pseudo-albino.
- Buckskin of any shade is best crossed with deep red bay, so no cremello or perlino is produced.
- Buckskin crossed to a bay or brown which has never produced a chestnut foal will reduce the chances of palomino and chestnut.

The true buckskin is a single dilute colour, formed by the pairing of the *Cremello* allele C^{cr} with bay or brown. Until the formation of the Buckskin registries, this colour was known in Australia as 'creamy with black points'. The shades of buckskin that may be identified (from lightest to darkest) are:

- **Cream buckskin** Off-white with a slight golden tint in sunlight and black points including ear tips.
- **Standard buckskin** Yellowish body colour with black mane and tail, and black legs (can have white markings) which characterise all buckskins.
- **Golden buckskin** A deep gold, almost orange body colour highly prized for its attractiveness. Some may be so rich in tone as to be difficult to distinguish from copper bay, however, they are lacking in the 'redness' that even the lighter bays exhibit. A good coated buckskin will glisten gold or metallic silver in sunlight, whilst a bay will glisten copper or orange.
- **Sooty buckskin** This is the common term but it is also known as mouse, burnt buckskin, and brown buckskin. The sootiness is due to the darker base colour, brown, and/or the action of the sooty allele on bay. The yellow is much more obvious than in the true brown.
- **Black buckskin** (also known as **dilute black**) Off-black, rusty or slate all over. The dilute black is the darkest member of the buckskin family. It is sometimes referred to as smoky, or occasionally

in Europe as the 'yellow-eyed black'. It is characterised as being an off-black or smoky shade of black, but in rough coat may be inadvertently classed as liver chestnut by the inexperienced, or mistaken for dun or brown. Each is incorrect. It is sometimes barely distinguishable from a true black horse. For this reason some buckskin registries do not recognise it. Readers will find that after looking at one or two of these, and 'getting their eye in', the distinction is not so difficult, except in extreme cases.

Fading black is diluted more strongly than non-fading black. Very rarely C^{cr}, although present, fails to affect black at all, due to non-penetrance of the C^{cr} gene. Such individuals cannot be distinguished from true black. To determine the genotype of such horses, look at the breeding history or background. Black buckskin may be mistaken for liver chestnut due to fading, although parting the hair will usually reveal a dark smoky undercoat.

Identifying black buckskin
How does one know if an apparently black or near-black horse is actually a black buckskin? For registration purposes, this can sometimes be difficult, but Buckskin classifiers will discuss this with you and make an evaluation. If a decision cannot be made simply by looking at your horse, because

of indifferent coat condition or other reasons, breeding background must be taken into account. Knowing that to be a black buckskin a horse must have C^{cr} in its genotype we can discount all purebreds of certain breeds.

Pure draught breeds, Thoroughbred, Arab and many pony breeds can be considered free of C^{cr}. Most commonly the colour is found in the Australian Pony, Australian Stock Horse, Connemara, Quarter Horse, Shetland, Welsh Pony, and the miniature breeds. If the horse in question has a cremello or perlino parent it *must* be a black buckskin. If, to a normal base-coloured mate (bay, brown, black or chestnut) it produces a palomino or buckskin foal, it must be a black buckskin as well. A pseudo-albino from a palomino or buckskin mate is also proof. Finally, colour at birth is a definite guide, if this is known.

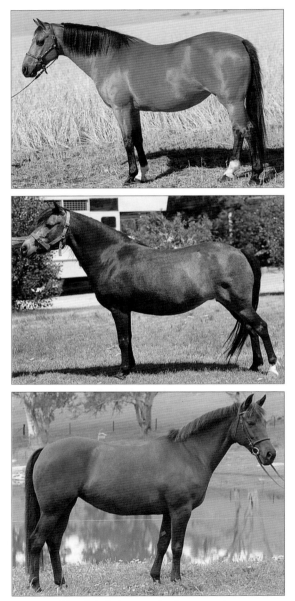

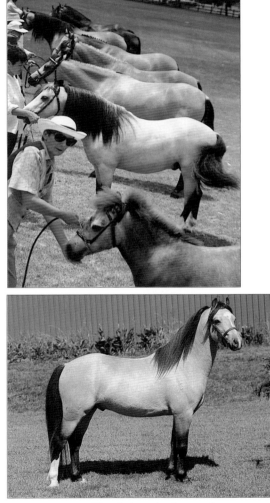

TOP: *A range of buckskin shades, with mouse buckskin in the foreground and cream buckskin behind that.* BOTTOM: *Standard buckskin Welsh Pony Berry Park Dwyn*

TOP: *Golden buckskin Australian Stock Horse Miss Tiffla.* CENTRE: *Sooty buckskin, part-bred Australian Pony Cotswold Twinkle.* BOTTOM: *Black buckskin or dilute black Australian Riding Pony Springtime Penny Royal*

The true black buckskin is born pale; as a foal it is mouse, fawn, pumpkin or butter-coloured and darkens at first change of coat. Black, on the other hand, will be born blue-black, or more commonly slate, brown or dark bay.

BREEDING BUCKSKINS

All dilutes, no matter what their sire or dam, are produced by the mechanism of incomplete dominance. One must not breed two dilutes together if wishing to avoid breeding the pseudo-albino. The breeding of two buckskins together, even the very darkest, the black buckskin, may result in cremello or more often perlino (25 per cent). For this reason it is considered good practice to breed all buckskins to a base colour. The chance of producing buckskin remains the same (50 per cent) as breeding two buckskins together.

There are many good quality bays, browns and blacks of the recognised pure breeds that can be crossed with buckskin for type and temperament improvement. Select a stallion that has never produced a chestnut foal (E^+E^+) for indication of homozygosity. An A^AA^A bay is ideal because this gives the classic deep gold buckskin. Perlino or cremello bred to a homozygous bay will give buckskin 100 per cent of the time. Buckskin bred to buckskin can give all shades of buckskin, palomino, bay, brown, black or chestnut (trihybrid cross of $A^AA^aC^+C^{cr}E^+E^e \times A^AA^aC^+C^{cr}E^+E^e$).

It is possible to produce palomino from buckskin. Some buckskins contain chestnut in their genotype, allowing palomino production (often

This black buckskin mare, Tammy (breeding unknown), was originally thought by her owners to be a chestnut because of her reddish appearance in winter coat. The locals thought she was liver chestnut, or maybe a brown. She was bred to a red chestnut and produced a palomino. We know that chestnut to chestnut always produces chestnut, so the mare could not have been a genetic chestnut. This pony is shown in summer coat on page 126

Popular crosses for producing buckskin

Buckskin bred to buckskin:
$C^+C^{cr} \times C^+C^{cr} = C^+C^+$ (base colour, usually bay) 25%, C^+C^{cr} (dilute, usually buckskin) 50%, $C^{cr}C^{cr}$ (pseudo-albino, usually perlino (25%) (rule 4, line 4, page 13)
Bay bred to buckskin:
$C^+C^+ \times C^+C^{cr} = C^+C^+$ (base colour, usually bay) 50%, C^+C^{cr} (dilute, usually buckskin) 50% (rule 2, line 2, page 13)
Bay bred to perlino:
$C^+C^+ \times C^{cr}C^{cr} = C^+C^{cr}$ (dilute, usually buckskin) 100% (rule 3, line 3, page 13)

---

because such buckskins have themselves been bred from a palomino parent.) Many of these buckskins are readily distinguished by the fact that, at the base of their tail, and sometimes in the mane, they carry a sprinkling of white hairs, called 'frosting'.

The action of the diluting gene is to lighten all brown or reddish pigments to yellow or gold, while black remains unaltered. Hence, bays with rich black legs leave buckskins with rich black legs. Bays with lesser black tone leave buckskins with tan or chocolate legs and sometimes brown manes and tails. These are known as 'seal points' and generally come in standard or cream shades. Dorsal stripes and other markings are no more prevalent on buckskins than on horses of other colours and are in no way an identifier of the horse as a buckskin. A dorsal stripe, and occasionally leg barring, may even appear on some Thoroughbred horses, which of course cannot be buckskin. A more complete discussion of dorsal stripes and the whole range of primitive markings will appear in the next chapter on duns.

Can the buckskin ever become a breed?

By definition a buckskin is a single dilute, and is heterozygous, C^+C^{cr}. No matter how many generations of buckskin breeding are in the pedigree, a buckskin individual can never be pure-breeding. The test of any breed is that it must be capable of breeding true to type. This is no less true of the colour breeds. Buckskin and palomino are colours that are incapable of reaching purity. For this reason no breed of buckskin or palomino horses has ever evolved. Custodians of these groups can be considered colour registries, not breeds. The ancient Akhal-Teke breed is most noted for its metallic golden buckskin colour, but all colours, including palominos and perlinos, are found in this breed.

9

THE DUNS

Quick Guide: Dun

- The four categories of dun are red, yellow, mouse and blue.
- All the many and varied names for different duns are simply specialised terms based on local/regional or breed use.
- Duns have minimal iridescence, and always have a prominent dorsal stripe, mask and leg barring, known as primitive markings.
- The dunning gene lightens out the body of the four base colours and leaves primitive markings the same colour as the mane and tail.
- The dunning gene is dominant so its presence is visible and affects all base colours.
- Dun bred to dun usually produces dun (75%), but chestnut, bay, brown and black are also possible. Pseudo-albino is not possible.
- Individuals that produce 100% dun have two dun parents.
- Yellow dun (dun mechanism) and buckskin (cremello mechanism) are frequently confused as one and the same.
- Buckskin associations include all duns as well as buckskin under their umbrella.
- There are several breeds of dun.
- The native colour of the Fjord, a specialised breed of dun horse, may be the result of a different allele.

These very unusual, attractive horses are the result of a different dilution mechanism. Duns are controlled by the dominant dilution D^D, which alters the concentration of pigment to one side of the shaft of the hair. This causes a high degree of translucency on the other side and gives the coat its characteristic diluted appearance. The individual granules of pigment are more nearly normal in size and shape than are those of C^{cr} heterozygotes. Duns may be $D^D D^D$ or $D^D D^d$. Non-duns carry the allele for non-dunning recessively as $D^d D^d$, thus following Mendelian inheritance. No difference is seen in the outward appearance of pure-breeding duns from the impure or heterozygous dun.

DILUTING ACTION OF THE DUNNING GENE

The action of the dunning gene is twofold. First, it lightens the base colour. Reds are converted to apricot, yellow or peach; liver is converted to bronze or mud colour; brown is converted to rust or 'wolf'; and black is converted to slate (gunmetal grey) or ashen blue. This lightening process does not appear to affect the legs unduly, or the front of the face, leaving a darker 'mask'. There is also a great deal of variation in the size and contrast of the mask. Second, it gives the primitive markings discussed on page 41.

Genotypes of the duns

$D^D D^D$ or $D^D D^d$ + bay = Yellow dun (standard)
$D^D D^D$ or $D^D D^d$ + brown = Mouse dun (dark)
$D^D D^D$ or $D^D D^d$ + black = Blue dun or grullo
$D^D D^D$ or $D^D D^d$ + chestnut = Red dun (also liver, bronze, copper, apricot, peach)

The main shades are, from lightest to darkest: standard yellow dun, mouse dun, blue dun or grullo, and red dun.

Standard yellow dun

The body colour is dull yellow or tan, the face is masked by darker yellow or reddish-tan, with black mane, tail and primitive markings. Sometimes the face masking is limited to an indistinct darker shadow down the bridge of the nose.

Unlike the standard buckskin, yellow dun is usually dull and lacking the iridescence that often accompanies buckskin. This is the classic yellow dun that is frequently confused with standard buckskin. Cream dun is cream or off-white, somewhat like the cream buckskin.

The variations are due to the wide variety of shades of bay which D^D is acting upon, and the *Sooty* factor (*Sty* allele). Yellow dun bred to yellow dun is a trihybrid cross of $A^A A^a D^D D^d E^+ E^e$ × $A^A A^a D^D D^d E^+ E^e$ (see Table B, page 134) and gives all shades of dun, as well as all the base colours. Yellow dun is best produced by breeding yellow duns together, or by breeding yellow dun to bay.

Mouse dun

A dull, rather nondescript, darker shade of dun, more mud-brown or tan than yellow, with distinct mud-brown face mask and black primitive marks, produced by the action of the dunning gene on brown. This is sometimes known as olive grullo, muddy grullo or wolf dun.

Blue dun or grullo

Essentially the grullo (pronounced gru-yo) is a diluted black horse. It has the appearance of a clipped-out black, except for the legs and head. Each individual hair is diluted out, rather than being an admixture of different coloured hairs found in other colours, such as the grey.

Another feature is the black dorsal stripe which is a prerequisite for the grullo. This is very distinctive, running into both mane and tail hairs, either side of which are diluted hairs. A shoulder stripe or shadow and black leg barring are always present.

The grullo can range from a light gunmetal silver which often shows iridescence (silver grullo), to slate grey, blue (lobo dun) to faded blue-black.

Grullo is the Western breed term, from the Spanish *grullo* ('crane') referring to the blue-grey colouring of the native crane. The Europeans have always referred to the colour as 'blue dun'. Either term is correct, hence we may find blue dun Connemara Ponies and grullo Quarter Horses (where the grullo is known as 'grulla'). It is claimed by some breeders that grullo is the rarest form of

---

> **Shades of red dun (lightest to darkest)**
>
> | | |
> |---|---|
> | Light red dun (peach dun) | dominant |
> | Apricot dun | |
> | Red dun | |
> | Copper dun | |
> | Bronze dun | |
> | Liver dun (muddy dun) | recessive |

---

dun and by inference that it is therefore more valuable. They next claim that it is the 'strongest phase of the dun factor' as if to infer that its 'strength' makes it a goal of all dun breeders. These are misleading statements.

The truth is that the formation of grullo colouring relies first on the production of the genotype for a black horse, with the additional presence of D^D in the genotype. Because of selection, black horses are less common in most breeds than other base colours. Grullo will be correspondingly less common among the dun family.

The grullo has a lot to recommend it, for its dark skin and hardiness make it well regarded among the stock horse breeds.

Breeders desiring to produce the grullo should breed grullo to grullo which gives the best odds of producing grullo (75 per cent chance of the dihybrid cross $D^D D^d E^+ E^e$ × $D^D D^d E^+ E^e$—rule 4, line 4, page 13), but also gives black, red dun or chestnut.

The alternative is to select black horses and breed these to a grullo (50 per cent) (rule 5, line 5, page 13). If these colours are not available, any other heterozygous dun known to have produced black or grullo previously will be suitable. From other duns, the odds are lengthened.

Red dun

There are several types of red dun, all named as a result of a darker or lighter chestnut base colour. These are listed in the shaded chart above. The mane and tail varies from dark brown to light red, depending on the type of chestnut base colour. The flaxen mane and tail of some chestnuts is less commonly seen in the red dun, probably due to the effect of the dorsal stripe.

Light red dun is sometimes incorrectly called 'claybank dun'. In Europe, the red dun is frequently referred to as 'yellow dun with dun mane and tail'. Red dun is best produced by breeding red dun to red dun (75 per cent) or else red dun to chestnut (50 per cent).

The range of shades in dun: FAR LEFT: *Standard dun Highland Pony with 'barbs' off the dorsal stripe.* LEFT: *Blue dun (grullo, lobo dun) pony Akahl Serenade, dam of Akahl Babushka.* CENTRE LEFT: *Yellow dun with shadowing, part Arabian Akahl Babushka.* BOTTOM LEFT: *Grullo part Quarter Horse stallion Kalkadoon Shogun.*
CENTRE RIGHT: *Mouse dun with mottling and ghost striping.* BOTTOM RIGHT: *Silver dun (grullo) Welsh pony (photos far left, centre right and lower right, J. Wiersema)*

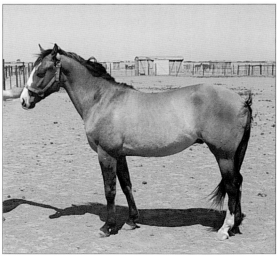

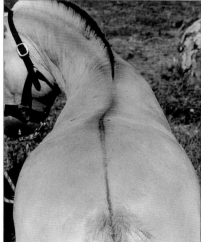

TOP: *Dark red dun.* ABOVE AND RIGHT: *The same horse showing striping on neck and zebra stripes on hocks*

ABOVE: *Light red dun (peach dun) Quarter Horse Wagas Red Terror* LEFT: *Divided and incomplete dorsal stripe*

SECONDARY ACTION OF THE DUNNING GENE

A secondary characteristic of the dunning gene is to produce 'zebra' or primitive markings, such as dorsal stripe and leg barring. Occasionally these markings will be present as a separate factor in ordinary coloured horses such as bays and chestnuts, but they are not as pronounced. Not all primitive markings need necessarily appear at the same time in an individual, but with rare exceptions a true dun will have the dorsal stripe, mask and leg barring.

Primitive markings
1. Dorsal stripe
2. Leg barring
3. Mask
4. Ear tips and ear edging
5. Shoulder stripe or shadowing
6. Neck striping or shadowing
7. Cobwebbing on face
8. Mane and/or tail guard hairs
9. Mottling

1. Dorsal stripe
The dorsal stripe may be black, brown or red, varying according to the base colour. A yellow dun by

definition has a black dorsal stripe. The stripe will run along the backbone from the withers to the base of the tail, appearing to run into the mane and tail. Occasionally, the stripe will not run the length of the back, or is divided. The more pronounced the stripe the better.

Dorsal stripes are also known as 'lineback'. The dorsal stripe is typically like a child's pencil drawing—perhaps a little crooked around the edges, or widening and narrowing as it progresses down the spine, or (rarely) broken so as not to form a continuous line.

The dorsal stripe of the dun matches the mane colour, so a red dun will have a red or brown dorsal stripe. This is helpful for identification, as some red duns look very similar to bay, which has a black stripe, if present at all.

2. Leg barring
Horizontal stripes of varying widths, the same colour as the dorsal stripe, across the hocks, forearms and knees are known as leg barring, zebra or tiger stripes. In many duns the lower leg is quite light and it is only the leg barring that makes the legs appear darker. Zebra stripes appear on the back of both the knees and hocks and, less commonly, across the fronts of the forearms or stifles. Rarely, more extensive stripes, barbs, or ghost markings (as seen on the photo of blue dun on page 40) can occur higher up the body, giving a brindle effect.

3. Mask
Black, brown or red will occur on the bridge of the nose with usually some colour around the eyes. The masking effect may spread to the jaw and muzzle, or as outlines around the lips and nostrils. Some-times the whole head and neck are dark. Masking is one of the most reliable indicators of the presence of the dunning gene. The mask is present to a greater or lesser extent in all duns, even those which carry a blaze or other white marking on the face. White markings are not excluded by the dunning gene, but dun breeders prefer horses without them so that the full effect of the dun character is displayed.

4. Ear tips and edging
Most commonly seen as darker colouring on the ear tips or the entire edge of the ear. Less common is the half or three-quarter dark ear. Again, this will match the dorsal stripe, so red tips will be found on the red dun.

5. Shoulder stripe or shadowing
Transverse stripe(s) over the withers running down from the wither in varying widths and lengths are known as shoulder stripes. In some cases, a large shadow effect is seen, due to the large area covered, or the stripes being close together.

6. Neck striping or shadowing
These are unusually dark areas through the neck extending into the hollow of the shoulder. Occasionally, dark shadows will appear only on the crest of the neck or dark lines will point down from the base of the mane.

7. Cobwebbing
Cobwebbing, sometimes known as 'chicken feet', occurs on the face and originates under the forelock. Lines extend in varying lengths over the forehead resembling a spider web. Occasionally, lines extend from the eye in a 'misplaced eyebrow' effect. Pencilling may occur completely around the eye. Many stripes are known as 'zebra face'. A dark patch may be present on the jaw or cheek bones.

8. Mane and/or tail guard hairs
Guard hairs are coarse white hairs along each side of the mane and across the top of the tail. These hairs are usually only a couple of inches long, and tend to stand upright.

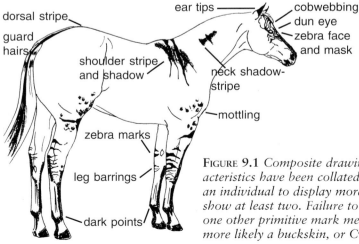

dorsal stripe
guard hairs
shoulder stripe and shadow
ear tips
neck shadow-stripe
cobwebbing
dun eye
zebra face and mask
mottling
zebra marks
leg barrings
dark points

FIGURE 9.1 *Composite drawing of primitive markings. These characteristics have been collated from various animals. It is rare for an individual to display more than four characteristics, but it will show at least two. Failure to exhibit the dorsal stripe and at least one other primitive mark means the animal is not a D-type dilute, more likely a buckskin, or C^{cr}-type dilute*

Guard hairs may be shed during the summer months and reappear during winter. Longer permanent white or cream hairs give a layered effect in the manes of some duns; these are known as 'sandwich manes'.

9. Mottling

Mottling appears as small dots or circles in shades darker than the body colour, and should not be confused with dapples. It is not generally found on the horse's winter coat. Mottling is found on the forearms, gaskins, shoulder and stifles.

TRUE BREEDING DUNS

The dun can breed true because homozygosity ($D^D D^D$) can be reached in the first generation. There are plenty of examples of dun stallions that have sired nothing but dun progeny of differing shades. Naturally, these stallions must have a dun sire and dam for this to occur. The original wild horse of Europe, the Tarpan, was always dun and most often blue dun. The Konik and Sorraia are dun, resembling the Tarpan. Breeds where the dun is common include the Connemara, Gotland, Highland, Icelandic Pony, Quarter Horse, Riwoche Horse, Spanish Mustang and Sumba.

THE DIFFERENCE BETWEEN YELLOW DUN AND BUCKSKIN

The breed term Buckskin is really a misnomer. The registries were originally set up to preserve the ancestral dun colours at a time when the inheritance of buckskin was not understood, and still include non-buckskins under their umbrella, specifically the duns.

Years ago yellow dun and buckskin were thought to be identical. However, the genetic colour definition of buckskin is a non-palomino dilute with a C^+C^{cr} genotype, whereas true dun has a $D^D\_$ genotype.

Confusingly, some buckskins do have a faint dorsal stripe—these are known as linebacked buckskins. This is possibly caused by an allele of the A series. However, the key to understanding the differences lies in the primitive markings.

The dunning gene creates primitive markings, which are always quite strongly marked. The dorsal stripe is bold—sometimes up to 5 centimetres (2 inches) wide. The essential feature is that even in poor coat, the dorsal stripe is pronounced, running along

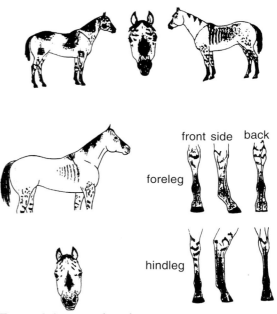

FIGURE **9.2** *Examples of primitive markings on dun horses (Courtesy ABRA)*

the spine into the mane and tail, which are bicoloured. Unless the points come so high in the dun as to obscure the primitive marks, all duns will have face mask and zebra stripes. Buckskins do not have the primitive marks.

An occasional horse will be a composite of both buckskin and dun, in which case the mask may disappear although the body colour is mainly unaffected. Looking at the pedigree of the horse is often an indicator which will allow you to distinguish between the two.

NATIVE DUN (*BLAKK*): NORWEGIAN FJORD PONY

Not included in the list of dun breeds so far is the Norwegian Fjord Pony, which is today exclusively dun. The Fjord's hair colouring is its most striking characteristic and the one which sets it apart from all other horse and pony breeds. Having been purebred in virtual geographic isolation for over 1000 years in its native country, it has retained many of the characteristics of the primitive horse, including the heavy upright mane (which may fall over if it grows long enough) and the primitive colouring. Bay and brown were also found until this century

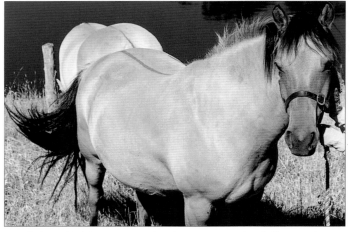

Mork brunblakk *in a crossbred. Compare the difference between this and the yellow dun non-Fjord at right (photo J. Wiersema)*

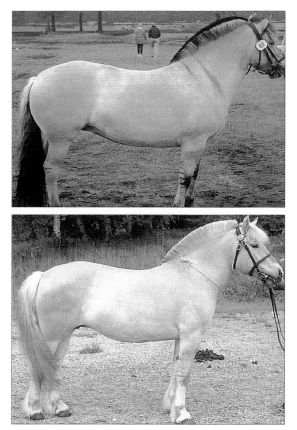

LEFT: *Ancestral dun in Przewalski's Horse*
BELOW: Gra *(left) and* brunblakk *(right), showing different coloured nose rugs*

TOP: Brunblakk *Fjord, showing primitive marks in two colours*
BOTTOM: Rodblakk

when the breed almost died out and now continues from the line of only one stallion.

The predominant colour is a straw-yellow shade, with pronounced dorsal stripe running into the centre of the mane and tail. These have very pale cream or white outer hairs (known as *klyping* in the mane and *bloom* in the tail). The dorsal stripe is almost always darkest through the mane, but may lighten elsewhere.

Occasionally the dorsal stripe is up to 2.5 centimetres (1 inch) wide. The forelock is always bicoloured, but sometimes there are more of the black hairs, making it look black from a distance, or there are more white or cream hairs, making the forelock look essentially fair. Sometimes the colours are balanced evenly.

The native colour is not unlike the colour of Jersey cattle with its varying shades of grey, red, tan and gold and its lighter soft parts. The mask (translated as 'nose rug' because it is most obvious on the lower part of the nose) is generally a soft reddish-brown, but may also be tan, gold or grey. There will be a light muzzle ring in all except the grey dun.

The remaining dun characteristics are not as strongly marked. The legs have darker smudges or black clouded effects, rather than the prominent points of other breeds, most often with an unusual cream circle around the coronary band, approximately 2 centimetres ($^3/_4$ inch) wide. There is sometimes a cinnamon smudge or freckles on the upper front legs, shoulder, cheeks or even the eyebrows.

While the points are less distinct, zebra markings are often visible on the hocks and knees, often more prominent on the sides of the leg and always symmetrical. Higher up on the forearms, zebra markings may be the same colour as the mask. Occasionally, a wither cross is present or transverse lines appear along the mane and neck. These are known as fork marks. White markings can occur, but are not encouraged because they are thought to reflect impure breeding in a pony's ancestry.

Five dun colours, in addition to the usual native yellow dun (*brunblakk*), occur in the Fjord pony: *rodblakk*, *gra*, *ulsblakk*, *gul* and *kvit*. The distinctions between them are not always clear-cut, particularly in view of the seasonal changes from light in winter to darker in summer. For identification and registration purposes, the Fjord should be described as native dun, with the colour of the dorsal stripe and other relevant primitive markings described.

Genotypes of the native dun in the Fjord Pony

Brunblakk: A^+, A^A or $A^t\_C^+C^+E^+\_D^+D^+$ = Bay/brown + dun

Gra: $A^aA^aC^+\_E^+\_D^+D^+$ = Black + dun

Rodblakk: A^+, A^A or $A^t\_C^+C^+E^eE^e D^+D^+$ = Chestnut + dun

Ulsblakk: A^+, A^A or $A^t\_C^+C^{cr}E^+\_D^+D^+$ = Buckskin + dun

Gul: $\_\_C^+C^{cr}E^eE^e D^+D^+$ = Palomino + dun

Kvit: $\_\_C^{cr}C^{cr}\_\_D^+D^+$ = Perlino/cremello + dun

At birth, the Fjord is very light with barely visible markings. One can nearly always see the dorsal stripe, however, unless it is one of the pale rodblakks. It is the leg markings and the smudges which do not show up until later, so much later that it may not be possible until spring of the following year to ascertain the correct colour. Any registration of the foal before change in foal coat could lead to error, so permanent colour should be evaluated after this time. Over the lifetime of the horse, the colour tends to become slightly darker anyway. Only these six colours, in decreasing order of occurrence, have been recognised by the Norwegian Stud Book since 1922.

Ulsblakk, *with loss of primitive marks due to the cremello dilution gene* C^{cr}

Brunblakk

The literal translation of *brunblakk* is 'brown dun'. This is the native yellow dun—brown-tan to straw-coloured with black stripe in the mane, which strangely changes to red along the spine, and cinnamon-tan mask. The tail will have cream and black throughout. It is the wild dun form of bay and brown and is the most frequent colour. Very dark brunblakk is known as *mork brunblakk* and looks similar to crossbreds, so may be a heterozygote. *Brunblakk* to *brunblakk* gives *brunblakk*, *rodblakk* or *gra*.

Rodblakk

Literally, *rodblakk* means 'fox dun'. This is the red dun—apricot-coloured, with not very strongly marked red through the mane, tail and primitive marks. It is the wild dun form of chestnut. *Rodblakk* to *rodblakk* always gives *rodblakk*.

Gra

Literally translated, *gra* means 'black dun'. This is the grey dun, or native blue dun—grey with black stripe and points. *Gra* is silver-grey, ashen or slate coloured with darker grey mask and an overall grey cast to the body as in Jersey cattle. It is the wild dun form of black and does not have the light muzzle ring. *Gra* can carry C^{cr} which is seldom detected in the phenotype, as occasionally *gra* to *gra* will give *kvit* (white). *Gra* to *gra* gives mainly *gra* or *rodblakk*.

Ulsblakk

Ulsblakk means, literally, 'wool dun'. This is the cream dun, also known as reindeer dun. It is a flat cream with black stripe in the mane and tail, and faint red stripe down the back, with little or no markings on the face and legs. It is the wild dun form of buckskin as it carries C^{cr}, so to another *ulsblakk* it can produce *kvit*. For this reason, *ulsblakk* fell into disfavour and is not often seen. *Ulsblakk* to *ulsblakk* gives all colours.

Gul

Gul means 'gold dun'. This is cream with a gold stripe in the mane and tail, and minimal gold in the points. Quite rare, it is the wild dun form of palomino. *Gul* to *gul* gives *gul*, *rodblakk* and *kvit*.

Kvit

Kvit means 'white'. It is a uniform off-white with barely distinguishable cream dorsal stripe and markings, with glass eyes. This is the wild dun form of perlino and cremello. Glass eyes are not welcomed in the breed. *Kvit* to *kvit* gives 100 per cent *kvit*.

Gul and *kvit* are rarely identified and may have disappeared from the breed altogether. They could easily be resurrected, if desired, by crossing *ulsblakk* with *rodblakk* or *ulsblakk*.

Of all horse breeds, the Fjord most closely resembles Przewalski's Horse. As with Przewalski's Horse, crossbreeding with Fjords produces an intermediate colour between the two parent animals, with darker body colour, dorsal stripe of the native dun, and no klyping or muzzle ring. This suggests that both klyping and the muzzle ring are recessive.

The Fjord pony may have lost the A^A and A^t alleles, thus A^+ would give it its light colouring. However, because of the unusual red dorsal stripe seen in the *brunblakk*, it appears more likely that in this breed the dun colour is the result of another allele of the dun series which is a remnant of the ancestral dun, D^+.

Crossbreeding tends to confirm the separate colour status of the Fjord pony. The distinction is merely academic, for in practice, it makes little difference.

10

TAFFY

Quick Guide: Taffy

- Taffy is the third dilution, which affects only black pigmentation.
- Bay, brown and black give the red, blue and silver dapple taffy.
- Silver dapple is a term that should be reserved only for those taffies with large full-bodied dapples and silver mane and tail.
- Taffy is a dominant gene.
- To breed a taffy one parent must be taffy.
- Black is the best colour for breeding the silver dapple, and deep red bay is the best colour for red taffy.
- Taffy bred to taffy gives mostly taffy (75 per cent) but chestnut, bay, brown and black are possible.
- Some individuals may produce taffy 100 per cent of the time, and these will have two taffy parents.
- Taffy is almost invisible on chestnut horses (red pigment) but if a chestnut is known to carry the taffy gene it should be described as chestnut taffy.

Taffy has brilliance of hue, a general hardiness and durability, and is attractive. Taffy, the third dilution mechanism, is more commonly described in the literature as the silver dapple, but I prefer the Australian terminology because it is all-embracing. All silver dapples are taffy, but not all taffies are silver dapples. The diluting action of the *Taffy* gene from the Z-series is unique because it affects black pigmentation more strongly than red pigmentation, which is affected only slightly. The areas of the horse affected are the black legs, mane and tail of the bay, for example, which will be altered to chocolate-tan in the legs and flaxen in the mane/tail. An all-black horse will be lightened to a pinkish dappled, palomino-like appearance, like a traditional child's rocking horse.

RED TAFFY

Red or bay taffy is bright reddish-orange body colour, free from any sootiness, with rich chocolate or tan points on the legs, and blonde mane and tail. Frequently, the mane and tail are streaked with silvery black hairs or, rarely, the blonde hairs are absent altogether. This type would best be described as 'bay taffy with dark mane and tail'.

The red taffy is sometimes confused with bay, or red dun, particularly if it carries with it a dorsal stripe (which appears from time to time in any colour). In poor coat condition, red taffy is often mistaken for chestnut with flaxen mane and tail.

BLUE TAFFY

This is a very dark, sometimes bluish colour, with orange-red highlights, particularly around the lower parts of the body. The body has large shadows of chocolate colour with, sometimes, some pale dappling through it. The mane and tail appear silver, but close examination reveals an admixture of blonde and black hairs. More rarely, the silvering of the mane and tail is limited to the tips, and the horse could best be described as 'dark taffy with dark mane and tail'. These are most unusual and the lay person could have difficulty identifying it.

SILVER DAPPLE

The silver dapple effect is well documented in the literature as a colour in Shetland ponies, under the

Close-up of shoulder of classic silver dapple taffy Australian Pony

Red taffy Australian Waler stallion Cobba at different times of the year

Red taffy with dark mane and tail, Australian Stock Horse Boonoonah Sieda

Light red taffy (breeding unknown). This colour is frequently mistaken for chestnut

control of series *S*, which is normally used for pie-bald spotting. Sponenberg (1983) prefers to assign it to series *Z*. The inheritance would be a simple dominant dilution mechanism, similar to that in duns, so one parent must always be a taffy. Breeders believe homozygotes do occur but these cannot be distinguished by appearance.

The classic silver dapple or taffy pattern is described as a sepia-brown body colour, flaxen or ivory mane and tail, flaxen extremities, particularly on the coronet and pasterns, and a most striking pattern of cream or flaxen dapples on the body. These usually remain regardless of nutrition or seasonal conditions. Sometimes they are as large as a fist, with the brown that forms the outline of the dapples looking more like veins of marble. The darker the black base colour the richer and more striking the silver dapples appear. The foal is born pinkish cream or biscuit-coloured, somewhat like

Blue taffy Australian Pony stallion Bieres Meyein

a palomino, with mouse-grey face. The dapples, however may be completely absent.

CHOCOLATE TAFFY

Those dark taffies which do not display the silver dapples are known as 'chocolate taffies'.

In the United States, the spectacular naturally-gaited Rocky Mountain Horse traces back to a single sire, Old Tobe, which was chocolate taffy. Some 30 to 40 per cent of the breed is now this colour. Although all solid colours are allowed, chocolate flax, as it is known in the United States, is the most highly prized colour.

CHESTNUT TAFFY

The taffy gene can be superimposed on a chestnut horse with barely any visible effect, although some have a 'fawn' dappled appearance. On liver chestnut the taffy may look dull smoky or chocolate-tan with silverish or flaxen mane and tail, easily mistaken for chocolate palomino and liver flaxen, but mane and tail are less 'clean'. Those with darker mane and tail may be mistaken for liver chestnut, or dilute black, but there are usually a few revealing light dapples on the lower legs or lower cheeks.

ORIGIN OF THE TAFFY

In their appearance these horses mimic chestnut, but to bay and black they can produce taffy. When the base colour is liver, they may mimic chocolate taffy. Where the genotype is known, they should be recorded as 'chestnut taffy'.

Bay taffy to bay taffy gives all taffies, bay, brown, black and chestnut. Dark taffy to dark taffy gives all taffies (except bay taffy), brown, black and

Taffy genotypes
Bay + Z^Z_ = Red taffy
Brown + Z^Z_ = Blue (dark) taffy
Black + Z^Z_ = Silver dapple or chocolate taffy
Chestnut + Z^Z_ = Chestnut taffy
Liver chestnut + Z^Z_ = Chocolate chestnut taffy

chestnut. Silver dapple to silver dapple gives silver dapple, black and chestnut. It is suggested that grey will lighten out more quickly in the presence of taffy and some will even be born near-white.

Silver dapple seems to have appeared in the Shetland Pony by mutation around 1886. Taffy also appears in Icelandic ponies, where it is known as *vindott*. Importation of horses into Iceland has been prohibited for some 900 years so the colour has been around for a long time.

The name taffy has probably come from the old descriptive term 'taffish', which means 'a good sort'

LEFT: *Chocolate flax Rocky Mountain Horse Mocha Royale*
BELOW: *Chestnut taffy Shetland-cross pony*

ABOVE: *Classic silver dapple Australian Pony*

Chocolate taffy Shetland Pony

or perhaps from 'Taffy', a colloquialism for Welshman. The colour has been in Australia for many generations, probably being introduced through Timor ponies, South African and Indian ponies. Indeed, Australian taffy owners generally believe their ponies go back to Timor blood. Certainly they all seem to carry a similar stamp of conformation and type.

Far from being rare in Australia, taffy is reasonably frequent and popular amongst the Miniature Horse, Australian Pony and Australian Stock Horse breeds, and is well known among Coffin Bay Pony lines and the Waler.

I am surprised its popularity has not inspired someone to start up a colour registry for it—there seems to be a registry for just about everything else! Worldwide, the colour features most notably in the Connemara, Dutch Warmblood, Falabella, Groningen Horse, Icelandic Pony and Shetland. An occasional blue taffy has been recorded in the Friesian.

The taffy is one of the most poorly described and recognised colours. I have seen a classic silver dapple horse advertised as palomino in an American Quarter Horse magazine, and a geneticist show a slide of a bay taffy as an example of a chestnut horse. Because of errors in description, breed registries have had to contend with problems of the occasional black or bay horse being foaled from so-called chestnut parents, or a taffy from a so-called bay and a chestnut parent. *Identical, or similar, phenotypes in the horse may be brought about by different genotypes.* Chocolate taffy and chocolate palomino are examples of this, as are yellow dun and standard buckskin. Phenotypic

similarity has been a major obstacle in deciphering the inheritance of some colours.

Anterior Segment Dysgenesis (ASD)

In 1997, an incompletely dominant eye disorder closely linked to the *Taffy* gene was reported by Dr Ramsey of Michigan State University, in the United States, following a case study of some 800 horses, mostly of the Rocky Mountain Breed. ASD is a syndrome which involves a group of abnormalities in the development of the anterior portion of the eye. A few or a lot of these different abnormalities may be found in the AA horse, but rarely is there any functional visual impairment. This is because most of the abnormalities don't affect sight at all. ASD is not a disease but a non-progressive structural disorder present at birth which does not change over time. A few extreme cases are found with subluxated lenses and these appear to function normally even under saddle. The exception is the very rare, truly blind horse which has the same handicaps any blind horse has.

Normal horses are genetically free of the disorder (aa) although there is a 12% likelihood of genotypic error due to non-penetrance. These are actually heterozygotes termed 'silent carriers'. The heterozygote (Aa) is normally evidenced upon opthalmic examination due to the presence of retinal cysts.

The Rocky Mountain Horse Association and breeders are to be congratulated on their swift support of Dr Ramsey in his research and setting up of an Equine Eye Registry, and their initiatives of policy, breeding guidelines, and production of an explanatory video. ASD has been found by Dr Ramsey to occur in Bashkir Curlies, Miniature horses, Morgans, all the Mountain breeds, Shetlands, and Saddlebreds, and while ASD *can* be found in horses of other colours, the vast majority are of the taffy colour. Taffies with the whitest manes and tails have the highest incidence. The disorder is also found in humans and dogs.

Although it has yet to be reported in Australia, I believe this is only because any horses affected severely enough to be clinically examined would be rare and thought to be isolated examples. However, it would seem desirable for taffy breeders to take the responsible step of having their horses examined so that AA and Aa individuals are not bred together. Furthermore, breeding taffy to non-taffy virtually eliminates the possibility of producing an AA foal (the only time ASD can ever result in significant visual impairment).

11

COMPOSITE DILUTE COLOURS

Quick Guide: Composite Dilutes

- Combinations can occur of any of the three dilution mechanisms.
- Cremello combined with dun can give claybank dun, seal-point dun, and silver grullo.
- The combination duns, when bred together or with buckskin/palomino, can give the pseudo-albino, and are best bred to bay, to avoid the risk of producing a pseudo-albino.
- Taffy and dun combination gives the taffy dun.
- Cremello and taffy composite does not commonly occur, and even rarer is the triple combination of taffy, dun and cremello dilution.
- The double dilute composite is always a pseudo-albino.
- Some composites mimic other more common colours.

A composite occurs when the horse contains more than one of the dilution mechanisms C^{cr} (*Cremello*), D^D (*Dunning*) and Z^Z (*Taffy*) in its genotype. When C^{cr} and D^D combine, we get amber eyes and marginally lighter to pale primitive markings. It is not possible to describe every combination so the more common ones are presented here.

COMPOSITE DILUTE (C^+C^{cr}) AND DUN (D^D_)

The Dutch call these composites 'wild colour mouse, grey and red'. There is no equivalent English term.

Claybank dun
This is the dilute of the red dun (chestnut + C^+C^{cr} + D^D_). This dun ranges from pale straw to a yellow clay colour, with darker legs. The primitive markings are golden or tan. The mane and tail are mostly cream or white, except where the dorsal stripe runs through. Due to this, claybank dun is known as 'palomino dun' in Europe. Claybank bred to claybank gives claybank, red dun, chestnut, palomino or cremello.

Composite yellow dun (seal-point dun)
This is, in fact, buckskin or mouse buckskin and yellow dun occurring together (bay + C^+C^{cr} + D^D_). Yellow dun is not altered to any great extent by the

cremello dilution, other than changing the yellow body colour to flat cream. The primitive markings may be off-black or seal-pointed. Composite dun bred to composite dun gives any of the duns, base colours, dilutes as well as pseudo-albino.

COMPOSITE GRULLO

This is the dilute of the grullo or blue dun (black + C^+C^{cr} + D^D_). The composite grullo is not commonly identified, for it is frequently indistinguishable from normal grullo, other than being a flat cream or paler version. Some grullos in winter coat become very light anyway, so the only difference is in the breeding potential of the two colours. Composite grullo bred to composite grullo gives composite grullo, grullo, black, dilute black, liver chestnut or sooty palomino.

COMPOSITE DOUBLE DILUTE ($C^{cr}C^{cr}$) AND DUN (D^D_)

What happens when the cremello dilution is in double dose ($C^{cr}C^{cr}$/pseudo-albino) and combines with the dun mechanism (D^D_)? This composite is essentially still a pseudo-albino with classic pink skin, glass eyes and faint primitive markings.

LEFT: *Claybank dun Quarter Horse with tan primitive marks (chestnut + dun + dilute).* ABOVE: *Palomino dun, a subtype of claybank, with gold primitive marks*

ABOVE: *Taffy dun Welsh pony, no C^{cr} dilute (composite of liver chestnut + taffy + dun).*

Linebacked perlino

This is the double dilute of the yellow and mouse dun (bay/brown + $C^{cr}C^{cr} + D^D\_$). It appears similar to the perlino with minimal pigmentation: whitish-cream body colour, glass eyes, with mane, tail, dorsal stripe, mask and points rusty, peach or smoky-coloured. In Europe this is called 'perlino dun'.

Linebacked smoky perlino

The double dilute of the grullo (black + $C^{cr}C^{cr} + D^D\_$). It has a cream body colour, smoky mask, glass eyes, smoky mane, tail and points, with darker smoky primitive markings.

Linebacked cremello

Dun combined with cremello gives a colour barely different from straight cremello but a faint dorsal stripe is sometimes visible (chestnut + $C^{cr}C^{cr} + D^D\_$).

COMPOSITE TAFFY ($Z^Z\_$) AND DUN/DILUTES

Dilute taffy

The composite C^+C^{cr} with the taffy dilution produces a lighter variant of taffy. Evidence from a herd of Connemara ponies owned by Mrs J. Heard in Victoria (Australia) suggests that dark taffy is

---

Taffy composites

	C^+C^{cr}	$C^{cr}C^{cr}$	$D^D\_$
Bay taffy	Lemonsilla	Perlino	Taffy dun
Dark taffy	Lemonsilla	Perlino	Taffy dun
Silver dapple	Fawn	Perlino	Taffy dun
Chocolate taffy	'Chocolate palomino'	Cremello	Taffy dun
Chestnut taffy	'Fawn palomino'	Cremello	Taffy dun

The rare combination of the single cremello dilution with taffy and dun changes taffy dun very little except to flatten out the colour of the mask somewhat, with the mane and tail always white. The double cremello dilution with taffy dun is indistinguishable from the linebacked perlino.

---

diluted to a murky yellow colour, often called dun although without any primitive markings. This colour is also known as lemonsilla or 'cactus chestnut'. Bay taffy is diluted to seal-point lemonsilla (bay + $C^+C^{cr} + Z^Z\_$). When chestnut taffy is diluted by C^+C^{cr}, we get the 'fawn palomino', born a pale mushroom colour. The Shetland stallion shown on page 53 could best be described as fawn, never acquiring a true golden shade. I identified this horse on phenotype as having the taffy gene before there was evidence in any progeny. Several years later the owners let me know he had never sired a taffy foal, and were concerned about false advertising. Upon investigation, he had indeed had some bay taffies to black mares, but these had been mistakenly identified as chestnuts. The effect on

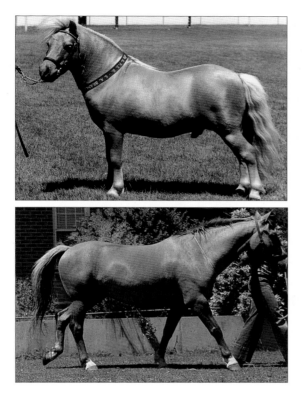

silver dapple taffy is much the same as on chestnut taffy, with fawn mask remaining on the head, although sometimes it appears bluish. Taffy combinations with the dunning gene produce a colour known as taffy dun. Taffy dun may mimic other colours depending on the base colour.

ABOVE LEFT: *'Fawn palomino' Shetland stallion Kipara Nugget (palomino + taffy).*
RIGHT ABOVE: *Lemonsilla (cactus chestnut) Connemara filly in front of dark taffy dam Tally (brown + dilute + taffy) (photo J. Heard).*
RIGHT BELOW: *Seal point dun, marks faded out, breeding unknown*
LEFT: *Lemonsilla (claybank mimic; no primitive marks) (red bay + dilute + taffy)*

Table 6.1 Relationships between dilute colours				
	BASE COLOUR			
MODIFYING ACTION	chestnut	black	brown	bay
Cremello dilution	palomino	black buckskin	dark buckskin	buckskin
Dun dilution	red dun	grullo or blue dun	mouse dun	yellow dun
Cremello and dun composite	claybank dun	composite grullo	composite yellow dun	composite yellow dun
Taffy dilution	chestnut taffy	silver dapple or blue taffy	dark taffy	red taffy
Taffy and dun composite	taffy dun	taffy dun	taffy dun	taffy dun
Cremello and taffy composite	fawn 'palomino'	fawn taffy	lemonsilla	lemonsilla
Double cremello dilution	cremello	smoky perlino	perlino	perlino
Dun and double cremello dilution	linebacked cremello	linebacked smoky perlino	linebacked perlino	linebacked perlino
Taffy, dun and cremello	Three factor dilute composite			

PART 4

COLOUR PATTERNS

The previous chapters dealt with the colour of horses. The next pages discuss the many patterns which can be superimposed on these colours, the result of genes which create white hairs.

Red ('liver') roan Welsh B pony mare Chiarini Daphne and foal (photo Y. Schafer)

12

GREY

Quick Guide: Grey

- The grey is a dark-skinned horse that progressively whitens with age.
- Grey is not a colour but a pattern superimposed over other colours.
- The base colour of a greying foal should always be recorded.
- A greying foal should never be described as roan.
- Grey is the result of a dominant gene that may mask all other colours.
- Two greys bred together may produce any colour recognised within the breed.
- A homozygous grey will produce 100 per cent grey and will have two grey parents.
- Grey bred to grey will produce grey (75 per cent) unless one of the parents is homozygous.
- Melanoma and pinkie syndrome are characteristic of many lines of grey horses. The incidence may be reduced by selective breeding.
- Speckles of the flea-bitten grey reflect the original base colour.

The grey has shown a remarkable resurgence in popularity over the last 90 years. Traditionally, greys in Europe were not common, kept mainly by the aristocracy for ceremonial purposes. This may have been due to the fact that the best horses, from the eighteenth century onwards, were the hotbloods, namely the Arabian and the Thoroughbred.

Greys were never popular among early Thoroughbred breeders and the colour almost died out until The Tetrarch came on the scene. Today, every grey Thoroughbred traces back to this horse. Similarly, until Skowronek left his mark on the Arabian, greys were nowhere near as common in that breed as they are today.

Probably the desire for hot blood meant that all colours not considered to be a hot-blooded colour were rejected as being novelties, gypsy or circus horses, or parade horses, certainly unsuitable as hacks or hunters for conservative England. This colour blindness did not seem to extend to ponies, however, where just about every second pony in some breeds seems to be a grey.

The grey colour is an admixture of white and dark hairs over the horse's entire body that progressively whitens with age. The skin is dark.

There appear to be three main types:

- The grey born dark with darker mane and legs, which lightens out slowly, possibly never becoming truly white;
- The grey born dark with white mane and tail, which also lightens out slowly; and
- The grey born light, which quickly becomes white.

Past writers have referred to grey as a 'disease'. Green (1974) refers to the colour as 'drying out': as the oils of the skin dry out in the surface layers, the roots of the hairs embedded in those layers dry out and the hair goes white, leaving those hairs embedded in deeper layers still coloured. Horses born darker colours (which generally have thicker hides) have most of their hairs embedded in the deepest layers and are not affected by the drying-out process until later in life.

I hear people say that they don't like greys, but don't mind a steel grey. This is a little naive, since all greys eventually go white. Greys are born some colour other than grey, but contrary to popular opinion they are not always born black. Any colour may turn grey if one of the parents is a grey. In reverse, grey may mask any other colour in its genetic make-up, as the greying gene, G^G, is epistatic (masking) to other loci.

Where the genotype of the grey is unknown, it is safe to say that two greys bred together can theoretically produce every colour known to exist in their respective breed.

GREYING OUT

There does seem to be a loose correlation between the colour the foal is born and how quickly it will grey out, but this is not infallible. The darker the foal at birth, the longer the process seems to take. Naturally enough, the colour of the parents will influence the colour the horse is born before it turns grey. Occasionally, a grey foal is born smoky and its base colour cannot be determined, because one of the effects of G^G is to add dark pigment to the coat, even in horses which are of genotype E^eE^e (chestnut). Normal chestnut-coloured greying foals may be born liver for this reason.

At birth, it is usually possible to tell by simple examination if the foal of a grey parent is going to be grey. The most obvious sign is the presence of white hairs around the eyelids, some so extreme that the eyes appear to be 'goggled'. The ears, muzzle, mane and tail hairs may show some white hairs or, very rarely, where no other sign is present, parting the foal coat near the hips and flanks will reveal white hairs in the undercoat. Since all greys whiten on the face first, then on the upper part of their bodies, most will show obvious signs in these places upon first change of foal coat. Goggled foals usually lighten rapidly. Occasionally one will become pure white in the mane or tail before the body is obviously affected.

Many grey foals with very plain heads or irregular facial markings change for the better, because the greying out process dresses up the faulty head, and hides the untidy blaze. Because of dark skin around the eyes, most greys give the illusion of having larger eyes than horses of other colours.

In 25 years of studying coat colour in horses, I have come across many extremes in the greying process. One filly was almost completely white upon change of her foal coat; another defied attempts to decide whether she was liver-ticked or grey. She stayed the same colour until she was five, but two years after that was a clear-cut dappled grey. Rapid and early greying is not an uncommon occurrence in the Arabian breed.

Another characteristic in some greys is the spots and patches, without underlying pink skin, that develop during greying out. These are known as 'watermarks'. The famous 'spotted wonder', The Tetrarch, had large fist-sized spots before he became white. Such greys give rise to the myth that they can be used in spotted horse breeding programs.

THE INHERITANCE OF GREY

The inheritance of grey in horses was one of the earliest colours to be studied and, as a consequence, geneticists are completely agreed as to its inheritance. Even before there was an accurate knowledge of heredity, Frederick Tesio, one of the world's greatest Thoroughbred breeders, had established the fact that a grey can occur only if one of its parents is a grey. Thus in theory every grey could be traced back in direct lineage to the original grey horse at the dawn of time, without ever skipping a generation.

Frederick Tesio (1958) analysed the Thoroughbred Stud Books and looked at every grey registered to that time. (No small feat!) This observation covered several thousand cases, but only 44 exceptions were found. It is significant that 36 of the 44 exceptions appear in the first four Stud Books when:

- It was difficult for the compilers of the Stud Book to obtain accurate data;
- These horses were never raced and their coats were never verified by the Racing Calendar; and
- Some were listed as having a 'roan' parent.

Tesio personally checked on five of the more recent anomalies and found that either one parent was a grey, but the change from birth colour had not been noted, or that in a few cases two stallions, one a grey, had served the mare in a season, but only the non-grey had been recorded. Tesio concluded every exception to be the result of error.

So infallible is the rule that a grey must have at least one grey parent that the keeper of the Australian Thoroughbred Stud Book will not even request blood typing evidence in support of such claims any more, for it is only wasting time and money checking out what is already known. (The same occurs with the rule that chestnut bred to chestnut always produces chestnut.) A foal can only be grey if it inherits G^G from one of its parents. If it does not inherit G^G but instead inherits G^+, the foal will never be grey. Additionally, since it does not contain G^G in its genotype it cannot pass G^G on to its own progeny. Once the greying gene G^G is lost, no more greys can be produced, until and unless one of these non-greys is bred back to another grey to reintroduce the greying gene. Stated another way, no matter how many grey ancestors a horse has in its pedigree, if it is not grey it cannot leave grey foals, unless and until it is bred to another grey horse (see Chapter 1, page 12).

Occasionally a homozygous or 100 per cent pure-breeding grey ($G^G G^G$) is produced. This can occur only if both the parents are grey, since only one G^G comes from each parent and two are needed for the homozygous blueprint. Once a homozygous grey is located, it is possible to 'fix' the grey colour within a strain by never outcrossing to a non-grey individual. The Percheron and Lipizzaner, and to a lesser extent the Andalusian, have reached the stage where the majority of their breed are in fact pure-breeding greys. This is particularly interesting in the case of the Lipizzaner, since the early foundation stock were all colours.

What happens if we breed two greys together?

If one of the greys is homozygous, or pure-breeding, all the foals will be grey. Some of these, approximately 50 per cent, will also be pure-breeding, but we could not be sure which ones until sufficient second generation foals were bred from the first foals (rule 2, line 2, page 13).

Only one non-grey foal is needed to prove both parents to be heterozygous (rule 4, line 4, page 13). The colour of the non-grey foal would depend on which genes were being masked by the impure parents. So two greys, bred from long lines of greys

over many generations, might still produce a non-grey foal. There is no guarantee of homozygosity until extensive breeding tests are carried out on a stallion, and it may be impossible to draw conclusions from a mare, owing to the small number of foals she would produce by comparison.

Note: The breeding of heterozygous greys has a 25 per cent chance of producing the pure-breeding grey. One can never be sure of the genotype of a grey simply by looking at it.

There appears to be no relationship between the rate of greying out and heterozygosity or homozygosity, although Bowling (1996) has suggested that flecked grey is more likely to be heterozygous, and pure white grey homozygous, in breeds which are mostly grey.

Registering a grey

Most breed societies now have regulations which require the colour at birth to be recorded on all greys. These are then recorded as 'grey foaled chestnut', or 'grey foaled buckskin', and so on. This is to try to eliminate 'unexpected' results from the breeding of greys. For registration purposes it is sufficient to describe a horse as 'bay or grey' if a decision between grey and bay is impossible.

Grey may also mask patterns such as spotting, tobiano or overo, which are evident at birth but fade through a blue and white stage ('shadow pinto'). The Argentineans call this *azulejo* after a South American bluebird. If in doubt, hose the grey down to see if the skin over the body is parti-coloured. A grey with a normal base colour will

Chestnut foal turning grey, showing goggles around the eyes and mouse grey muzzle

Grey Welsh mare with cremello foal. The sire of this foal was also a grey, but both parents were born a dilute colour, thus masking the C^{cr} genes in each parent. It is possible the cremello foal may still carry the grey G^G gene

have a dark skin over its entire body, but the shadow pinto will show patches of pink skin as well. (You may also find white socks and blaze.)

A grey parent, unknown to be carrying another pattern gene, may produce a patterned foal. This occurrence is responsible for the belief in some quarters that greys should always be bred to each other. If a grey was bred to, say, a bay, it was thought that one would get a bay and white pinto, or even a bay roan, as if somehow the colours had blended together. Nothing could be further from the truth.

Grey should never be recorded as an intermediate colour such as 'steel grey', 'blue grey', 'dappled grey'. Such descriptions are quite suitable for a horse's current identification, such as when a judge calls a 'rose grey' in from a line-up, but for registration purposes when a permanent colour is to be recorded, grey is the colour to list. Intermediate colours are only temporary.

A grey in its intermediate stage should never be described as 'roan'. This is very confusing and certainly misleading. True roan and the difference between it and grey are described in the next chapter. Just occasionally it is possible to find an individual containing both Rn^{Rn} and G^G in its genetic make-up. This is most likely to occur in ponies and Quarter Horses and is the only grey to be born genuinely roan.

DAPPLED GREY

A particular favourite is the dappled grey. These dapples are a product of the lightening process and are not related to nutrition, as are dapples in most other colours. The blue greys are most prone to exhibiting this trait. The dapples are dense on the lower half of the body; a rare horse will have large dapples over its entire body.

FLEA-BITTEN GREY

Some greys never go completely white, but rather appear to show a slight return of the original base colour in the form of speckles or flecking, known as 'flea-bites'. The colour of the speckles is a direct indication of the base colour of the grey, that is, its colour at birth.

Horses with red speckles would have been born a red shade such as bay or chestnut; horses born black would have black speckles. Yellow flecks

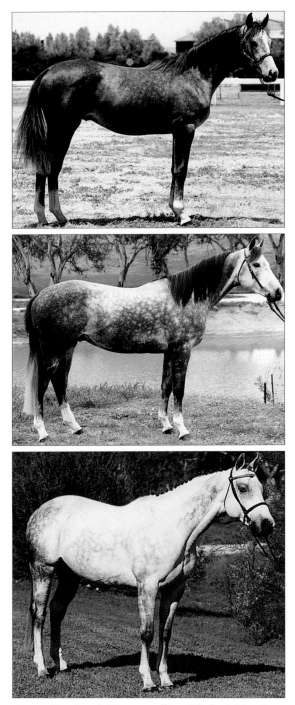

Australian Stock Horse stallion Chalani Mystic at 1 year (top), 4 years (centre) and 8 years (bottom), showing changes from dark grey, to dappled grey, to near white (mane still black)

would come from a horse born dun, palomino or buckskin. At this flea-bitten stage, any damage to the skin in the form of bites or cuts can result in darker speckles and spots forming on the site of the injury.

The earlier the speckles appear in the coat, the more concentrated and obvious they tend to become in older age. In unusual cases, the spots may be as large as a 10 cent coin, so that the horse resembles a leopard-spotted horse. Of course, the spotted characteristics of rat tail, mottled skin, striped hoofs and white sclera are not features of the true flea-bitten grey.

The flea-bitten feature is probably recessive, for it can occur from non-flea-bitten grey parents, even when only one parent is grey. This suggests that any non-grey can carry the gene for flea-biting (although not expressed) and that the factor is not linked to the greying gene. In Europe the flea-bitten grey is known as 'salt and pepper grey'.

Blood markings

Occasionally the flea-specks of the flea-bitten grey appear to concentrate in one area, forming a bold patch. So unusual and striking are these patches that legend has developed to explain their existence. The Arabs refer to them as 'blood markings', because of the resemblance to dripping blood. Most cultures develop explanations to solve the mysterious appearance of something unusual within their society, but of course the science of inheritance and genetics was completely unknown to ancient cultures. Blood markings have no doubt existed in one form or another since the beginning of horse history, and are depicted in old Chinese paintings as well as in more recent European works.

The patches may occur on almost any part of the body. Bloody shoulders and bloody buttocks are the most frequently encountered, but I have seen them on the neck, jaw, ribs and legs. One filly was particularly striking because of a bloody leg—the red patch was entirely on the inside of one front leg, making her appear to be permanently splattered with mud.

Blood markings are possibly inherited as a recessive characteristic which requires both parents to contribute the gene before the progeny can exhibit them. Since the markings often occur in animals with only one grey parent, the recessive gene could not be 'linked' with the greying gene. It will take a fairly unlikely chain of events to occur before we obtain blood markings, which accounts for the low frequency of the occurrence.

First, the presence of the greying gene is needed and this must be from a flea-bitten grey. (Blood markings only occur in flea-bitten greys.) Horse people generally believe the incidence of the flea-bitten grey to be much lower in any given breed than the ordinary grey, but no statistics are yet available on this point.

Then we need the particular recessive genes for blood markings. In all, one dominant gene (grey) is needed, then two pairs of recessives (flea-bites,

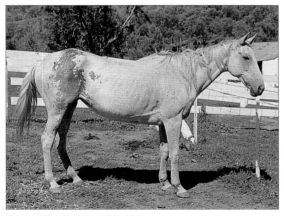

ABOVE AND LEFT: *Bloody buttocks on 'red' flea-bitten grey Thoroughbred, and close-up*

Black blood mark on 'black' flea-bitten grey

All-white grey Welsh A stallion Glangwesyn Poseidon

Pinkie syndrome

blood markings). The position of the marks appears to be at random but is likely to be controlled either by modifier genes or non-genetic factors.

DEPIGMENTATION

Throughout the life of a grey, pigment is removed from the hair and redeposited in the gut or skin, and this is thought to be responsible for the formation of the flea-bitten grey coat colour and the slow-growing deposits of pigment loosely termed 'melanoma'. Melanoma in grey horses should not be confused with skin cancer in humans which is malignant.

A large proportion of greys exhibit melanoma, even though its presence does not necessarily create any problem for the horse. Suggested figures show that as many as 30 per cent of all grey horses at the age of 16 years are affected. An abattoir worker told me that most greys he sees would have internal melanoma, though there may be no outward sign.

Melanoma seems to be more common in all-white grey than flea-bitten grey. Some breeders consider it is more common in greys that are dark at birth or whiten out slowly, but this is uncertain. Fortunately, simple selection procedures can reduce the incidence of melanoma considerably in grey × grey breeding herds, as some grey herds rarely show melanoma.

Further depigmentation, or pinkie syndrome, is common at any age in certain breeds such as the Lippizaner and Arabian, where skin pigmentation is lost especially around the eyes, and muzzle and occasionally the genitals and hooves. This can lead to photo-sensitivity, skin cancers and reproductive disorders. The intensity of the depigmentation can wax and wane but, on the whole, it is a problem which rarely shows permanent improvement and is thought be an inherited condition.

Dark skin is a characteristic of the grey, so its hide is very durable. The light coat has reflective qualities, which is an advantage in the sport of endurance riding. There are huge numbers of very successful greys in the sport, so much so that one could say that grey is the 'endurance' colour.

13

ROAN

Quick Guide: Roan

- Roan is a pattern of white hairs superimposed on the body but not the head and legs.
- It does not lighten with age, but may show darker pigmentation where there has been injury.
- It is evident in the first change of foal coat, if not already evident at birth.
- Roan is named after the base colour it is acting on, e.g. bay roan, black roan.
- Roan is caused by a dominant gene.
- Homozygous roan does not occur.
- Various types of ticking are often incorrectly called roan. These may be part of the roan family.
- Rare white striping may be a form of roan.
- In some breeds roan is part of a linkage group with chestnut and tobiano, and in others with bay.

The true roan has a fairly even mixture of white and base hairs throughout the body, but the head, lower legs, mane and tail remain the same as the base colour which identifies the type of roan. For example, a bluish body, brown head, black legs and mane or tail would be correctly described as a brown roan. The term 'blue roan' is no longer used, nor are 'red roan' or 'strawberry roan'. Instead, the base colour always precedes the word 'roan' so we have black roan, bay roan, palomino roan, grullo roan and so on. A rare roan will have white sprinkled on the jaws up to the cheek bones and in the tail.

DISTINGUISHING ROAN FROM GREY

In winter the roan coat generally lightens to almost white, but returns to the original colour in summer. This is a response to cold, or reduced daylight hours, and is probably a camouflage mechanism; a similar response is noted in some duns and dilutes and in other animal species. It is one way the true roan may be distinguished from a grey. A grey slowly whitens with age so that each winter the coat is lighter than

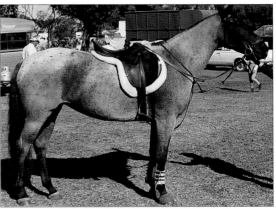

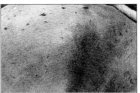

Brown ('blue') roan Australian Stock Horse Twist and close-up of flank.

the winter before, until the horse becomes completely white. Other roans, to confuse the issue, will darken in winter, and lighten in summer. It is not known if there is any genetic difference between these horses and those which go lighter in winter.

Roan and grey are the only colours in the horse where white hairs originate from dark skin.

INHERITANCE OF ROAN

A true roan is born roan, or is fully roan upon shedding its foal coat. It remains roan for the rest of its life. A grey is born a base colour and in its intermediate colour is still a grey. It should never be described as roan. The greying process in a true grey occurs firstly on the head and tail, so there is no need for confusion over the identification of roan or grey.

The dominant nature of the Rn^{Rn} gene means that only one parent need be a roan for roan to occur. Further, the genotype $Rn^{Rn}Rn^{Rn}$ is non-viable. Roan to roan does not produce dead foals, however. Rather, breeders suspect that the $Rn^{Rn}Rn^{Rn}$ embryo probably fails to implant, or is resorbed shortly after conception, in 25 per cent of roan to roan matings. Such an occurrence would go unnoticed since the mare would most likely come in season again and be rebred. If this were not so, we would expect to find roans with the $Rn^{Rn}Rn^{Rn}$ genotype whose offspring would be roan in all cases. The table opposite, given by Hintz and Van Vleck in the *Journal of Heredity* (1979, vol. 70) is of interest.

Roan occurs very frequently in draught breeds such as the Ardennes, Breton and Italian Draught Horses, as well as in the Welsh Pony, Australian Pony and Quarter Horse. It does not occur in the Thoroughbred, Arabian or Clydesdale. What is commonly referred to as roan in these breeds is not true roan, but ticking, heavy concentrations of white hairs throughout the coat. There is also confusion with the sabino pattern. Ticking is discussed in this chapter, sabino on page 71.

Nevertheless, an occasional roan individual with 100 per cent roan progeny has been reported in the Dutch and Brabant Draught Horses. It seems likely that such horses exist uncommonly, or they have other ticking patterns combined in their genetic makeup with a single Rn^{Rn} gene, and their progeny would be highly coloured with white hairs as a result of this ticking. In a breed which has been specially selected for roan as these are, such ticking would be heavy and easily mistaken for roan. The fact that so few 'homozygotes' have ever been reported tends to suggest an additional mechanism, such as ticking, at work in these horses, and that the exception proves

---

Roan and non-roan foals registered in 1937 from roan × roan and roan × non-roan matings in Belgian horses.

Type of mating	Progeny Roan	Non-roan
Roan × roan	130	67
Roan × non-roan	284	298

If homozygous roan is lethal, then the expected progeny ratio is two roan to one non-roan from roan parents [that is 2:1]. The actual ratio observed was 1.9:1

$Rn^{Rn}Rn^+ \times Rn^{Rn}Rn^+ = 25\% \ Rn^{Rn}Rn^{Rn}$, 50% $Rn^{Rn}Rn^+$, 25% Rn^+Rn^+ (rule 3, line 3, page 13).

If $Rn^{Rn}Rn^{Rn}$ was not lethal, we would expect 49 $Rn^{Rn}Rn^{Rn}$, 99 $Rn^{Rn}Rn^+$, 49 Rn^+Rn^+, that is, 148 roans, 49 non-roans. Because $Rn^{Rn}Rn^{Rn}$ is lethal, then the predicted 25% $Rn^{Rn}Rn^{Rn}$, 50% $Rn^{Rn}Rn^+$, 25% Rn^+Rn^+ becomes two-thirds $Rn^{Rn}Rn^+$, one-third Rn^+Rn^+, and we would expect 131 roans, 66 non-roans. These expectations are shown almost exactly by the reported results.

The expected ratio from roan × non-roan matings would be 1:1. The actual ratio observed was approximately 1:1.

(Reproduced by permission of Oxford University Press)

---

the rule. Another feature of the roan is the base-coloured speckles and spots that later develop. These are sometimes confused with Appaloosa spotting but are a result of injury, such as bites and cuts. Injury to a grey will result in lighter coloured marks. (An occasional exception to this will occur in the light flea-bitten grey, where injury can result in darker, more intense flea-bites.) Mottles on the lower half of the body of some roans, called 'corn spots' after the dark kernels on an ear of Indian corn, are not caused by injury, appearing spontaneously as the horse ages.

TICKING

Ticking is white hair, or flecking, intermingled throughout the coat. The amount of ticking in a horse increases with age; rarely are the white hairs evident at birth. Ticking is more common in chestnut than any other colour. There are two main types, both probably recessive alleles of the *Rn* locus. They are often mistaken for true roan, and occasionally sabino.

Coon-tailed ticking

This ticking is always associated with horizontal bands of white hairs on the top of the tail. Indeed, in some horses this may be the only sign that the ticking gene is present. In most cases the ticking is not very evident until the horse is mature, perhaps around five to six years of age and beyond, although I have had one obvious at birth. The white hairs or ticks are noticeable in the area around the flanks and belly, extending outwards in vertical bands up the ribs and over the hips. The heaviest concentration of white hairs is always around the flanks and lower half of the body. It is seen most commonly in Arabians and Thoroughbreds and breeds descended from these. Coon-tail is also known as *rabicano*, which translated from the Spanish means 'brush-tail'.

Standard ticking (Birdcatcher ticking)

The most common form of ticking, this is almost a reverse of the coon-tailed form. There are no bands of white hairs through the tail and the heaviest concentrations of white hairs are over the horse's top line (croup, hips, back, withers and occasionally the mane and head, where this colour has been referred to as 'self roan'). Generally, the white hairs are spread more extensively over the horse's body than in the coon-tailed tick. The flecking is rarely heavy enough to take on the 'white' appearance that a true roan takes on, nor is there sharp contrast between the colour of the head and the rest of the body. Birdcatcher ticking was named after the Thoroughbred Birdcatcher, which was reputed to have this form of white flecking. Its presence is the reason some Thoroughbreds have incorrectly been called 'roan'.

The colour is seen most often in chestnut Welsh Ponies and Arabians, where it is called 'armabi'.

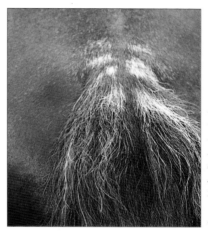

Banded tail of coon-tailed tick Australian Stock Horse stallion Master Herbert, (also shown on page 25)

Translated, armabi means 'hare-ticked'. Arabian breeders believe this pattern is associated with the Mesaoud bloodline. Heavy ticking is also seen in many draught breeds, and breeds descended from these.

Frosty roan

Sponenberg (1983) describes a particular form of ticking which he calls 'frosty' and he suggests it may be a variant of standard ticking or possibly roan. This consists of white hairs around the bony prominences such as hips and spine. I have not seen this pattern in Australia, which tends to indicate that the pattern may be a rare allele of the Rn^{Rn} locus.

CASE STUDY: ROAN THOROUGHBREDS

Many Thoroughbreds with white ticking have been called 'roan' over the years but no true roan has been recognised by the Australian Stud Book. A very

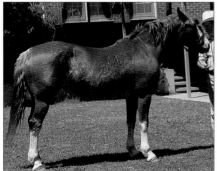

Chestnut marginal sabino with coon-tailed ticking

Welsh B pony with standard ticking

interesting case involves a stallion foaled in 1982, aptly named Catch a Bird. Catch a Bird is by Noble Bijou (Vaguely Noble × Priceless Gem) from Showy Countess (Show-off II × Sleepy Countess).

Catch a Bird was sold through the New Zealand yearling sales for NZ$ 90 000, and was described by the press as a 'zebra-striped colt from Serengeti'. Of course, the colt was not from Serengeti, and the stripes were in fact nothing like those of a zebra. The 'stripes' were vertical rows of white spots without underlying pink skin, joined like stripes primarily over the ribs and hindquarters. (A zebra is striped horizontally over the hindquarters.) Other white-striped horses of unknown breeding have been observed in the past, and these should not be confused with 'brindling' or zebra markings.

Catch a Bird was a good race winner himself and now stands at Harrington Thoroughbreds, Narrogin, Western Australia. At the age of 17 years he still has white stripes which have not changed over time. Interestingly, from a breeder's point of view, Catch a Bird has sired almost 40 foals from four foal crops, of which four foals have been born bay roan! (All from chestnut mares.) The oldest of these is a filly, Odd Colours (1992) from Out of Season by Trenton (imp.Argentina). Another, Slip Catch (1993), is a filly out of Golden Belt by Bletchingly. These are true roans on phenotype, confirmed by bloodtyping, but were registered in the Australian Stud Book as bays with ticking. (The Thoroughbred industry is not set up to register tricky colours.) The third roan is an unnamed colt born in 1994 from Policy Park by Lush Park. The last is a colt (1996) from Weston Gateway by Best Weston.

Originally it was thought that Catch a Bird's striped markings were some form of Birdcatcher ticking. However, the evidence of the progeny proves that Catch a Bird is unique. He has never left progeny of his own pattern. The roan progeny are all bays showing roan at birth, and the only changes have been a few dark patches that have developed over time, typical of the roan phenotype.

Evidently some change has occurred in Catch a Bird's sperm cells. His own colour is a 'one-off' (perhaps this is a true mutation, or a genetic stress response), but it has resulted in a genetic change which is visible in some of the progeny. Time will tell if the change to roan is genetically Rn^{Rn} with lethal homozygous effects as in normal roan, or some other mechanism.

Is there a relationship between ticking and roan? Given the Catch a Bird phenomenon, it is highly likely that this is the case. In recent years, investiga-

tion in the laboratory has discovered that a linkage exists between the loci for roan, tobiano and chestnut in paint horses. As all types of ticking are seen more frequently in chestnuts, it is likely that both ticking and roan are alleles of the Rn locus.

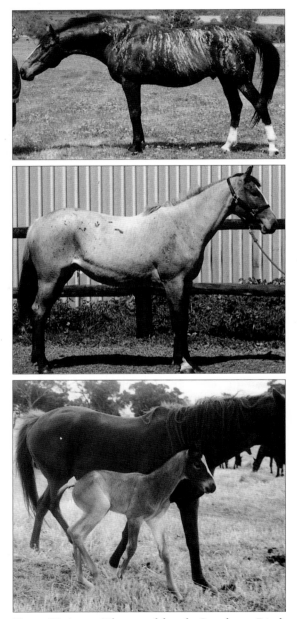

TOP: *Unique Thoroughbred Catch a Bird.*
CENTRE: *Odd Colours, daughter of Catch a Bird.*
BOTTOM: *Odd Colours as a foal, perhaps the first genuine roan Thoroughbred to be born in modern times*

PART 5

BROKEN COLOURS

White patches in the horse are a result of underlying pink skin leaving the hair devoid of pigment. Collectively, patched horses are known as pintos.

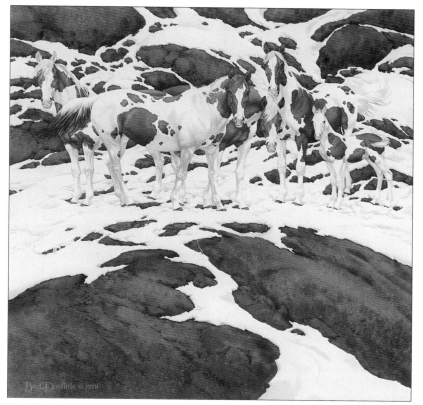

Guardian Spirits © *Bev Doolittle. Courtesy of The Greenwich Workshop, Inc., Shelton, CT. For information on the limited edition fine art prints by Bev Doolittle call (US) 203/925 - 0131.*

14

TOBIANO

Quick Guide: Tobiano

- Tobiano is a dominant pattern of white patches which appears to spread vertically down from the spine, and upwards from four white legs.
- Face markings are the same as on normal horses.
- Tobiano must have one tobiano parent, even if incompletely marked.
- Homozygous tobiano will produce 100 per cent tobiano, and have both parents tobiano.
- Bloodmarker analysis is now available to detect homozygosity in a potential breeding horse.

By far the most easily recognised pinto is the tobiano. The others are sabino, overo and splashed white. With a little observation and practice it is easy to distinguish and identify most examples.

Strictly speaking, tobiano (pronounced to-bee-ar-no) and any other broken colour or pied appearance is not a colour, but a white pattern interacting upon any one of the normal base colours, duns, dilutes, taffy, roan or grey. The terms 'skewbald' and 'piebald' are obsolete, for they do not give an indication as to the type of white marking present on a pied horse, nor its genetic make-up. Instead we now talk of black tobiano, grey tobiano and so on.

A major feature of the tobiano is that white will appear to start somewhere along the spine (generally neck, withers, rump or tail, in which case the tail will be two-coloured—rarely will other pinto types have a bi-coloured tail) and descend vertically. In a few cases the white may only be seen in the tail or withers, and on the legs. This is the only pinto colour that can have a dark head without white on it.

More frequently the white will cross the spine in at least three places. If it extends (descends) deep enough, the white will join up with the white of the legs. In very white horses, the colour is reduced to patches known as 'shields'. These commonly occur on the breast, flank, head and buttocks. The shielded tobiano is very susceptible to skin cancers in areas with limited protective hair covering such as the anus and penis. I know of no all-white

Features of the tobiano

- Body white crosses the spine;
- Body white appears to descend vertically;
- Four white legs with irregular edges;
- Ermine spots with dark hoofs;
- Patches of colour around the chestnuts.

Footnote to table

Of course there may be individuals which are exceptions in one of the above areas, but these have a preponderance of other features which still identify them as tobiano.

tobianos. Even where colour is reduced to the extreme, some colour always remains on the head. This is nature's attempt to protect the eyes. These individuals are known as 'medicine hat' tobianos.

The tobiano is a relatively simple pattern, for the colour is inherited as a simple dominant in true Mendelian fashion. Tobiano horses are $To^T To^T$ or $To^T To^+$, whilst normal-coloured horses are $To^+ To^+$.

The modifying genes which control the extent of the white markings in the tobiano are probably present in all horses, but rely on the presence of To^T to express themselves. Modifying genes are minor genes which occur independently of the major genes, and can only express themselves in the presence of a major gene. The chestnut Australian Stock Horse stallion Rannock (page 19),

FIGURE **14.1** *Gradients of tobiano*

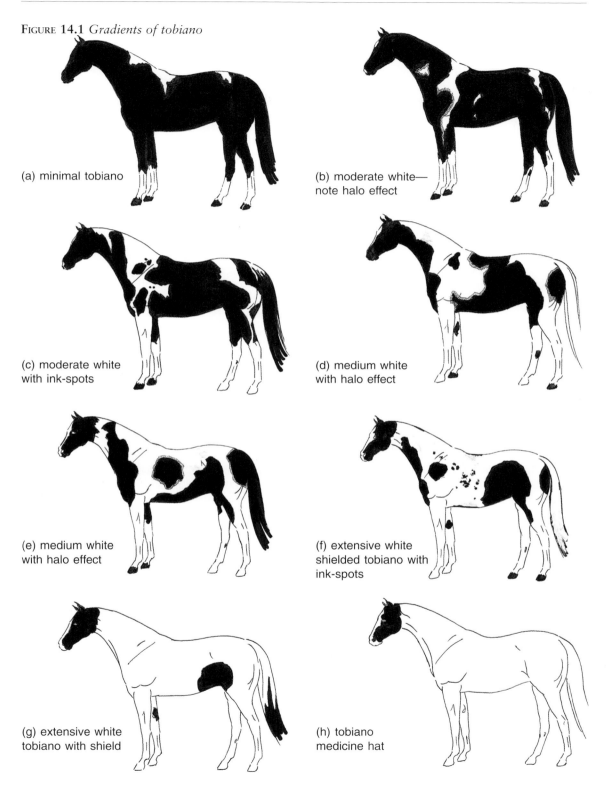

(a) minimal tobiano

(b) moderate white—
note halo effect

(c) moderate white
with ink-spots

(d) medium white
with halo effect

(e) medium white
with halo effect

(f) extensive white
shielded tobiano with
ink-spots

(g) extensive white
tobiano with shield

(h) tobiano
medicine hat

which we stood at stud, was bred on five occasions to tobiano mares of varying degrees of white, and all five resultant tobiano foals were of an almost identical shielded pattern, a result of modifying genes from their sire. It is thus possible to select individuals with pleasing patterns of white and so 'fix' the desired pattern in a breeding program.

Interestingly, the tobiano marking tends to be relatively symmetrical on each side of the horse's body. In 'best marked pinto' classes, it is usually a tobiano that catches the judge's eye. When I am judging a 'best marked' class, I will look for a horse that has roughly equal white and colour. As well as pleasing placement of the white, I look for dark hooves and strategic placement of the base colour so as to give maximum protection to sensitive areas.

The tobiano gene causes white to appear on all four limbs except in most unusual cases, which have two or more dark legs. Unlike normal socks or stockings, ermine spots are present on the coronary band, giving a black or partially black hoof. Stockmen consider the normally dark hoof of the tobiano to be an advantage over other colours with white markings and a white hoof. However, the genes for normal white markings can also be present in the tobiano. Under these circumstances, the foot will be white without ermine spots.

Another characteristic of the leg marking of the tobiano is the irregular finish to the top of the white. Rather than a 'spear' running up the front of the hock, it will run up the back or side, with a straight-cut edge. If white runs above the chestnut, the chestnut itself may be encircled by a coloured patch known as a chestnut patch.

Sometimes secondary spotting, also known as 'ink spots' or 'paw prints', is seen within the white areas. These are small dark spots surrounded by a roan area, such that the spot looks dark in the

UPPER LEFT: *A group of tobianos (photo D. Childs)*
UPPER RIGHT: *Black tobiano, minimal white. Note the large ermine spot on the off foreleg, ermine spots on the other legs, and the irregular edges to the 'socks'*
ABOVE LEFT: *Part-Arabian chestnut tobiano stallion Rondoro Capri. Note the chestnut colour forming a patch around the chestnut on the near foreleg*
ABOVE RIGHT: *Chestnut shielded tobiano, Australian Stock Horse Fascination*

centre, fading to white as it radiates out. Some shields also have a blurred or roan edge rather than a sharp-cut distinction, so that colour appears to bleed into the white. Face markings are not affected by the tobiano gene and will look like those of any other horse. However, one or both eyes may be wall-eyed. There is a higher incidence of wall eye in pintos than in solid colours. It does not carry over to non-pinto relations so, as geneticists would say, the wall eye is a pinto characteristic with low penetrance.

BREEDING THE TOBIANO

The tobiano is easily bred by selecting one tobiano parent to introduce gene To^T into the breeding programme. It is possible to find homozygous (To^TTo^T) pure-breeding individuals, but it is not possible to distinguish these by appearance. Some breeders believe that horses with ink spots will be homozygous tobiano (100 per cent producer) and indeed there is a high correlation.

Since pure-breeding tobianos are relatively uncommon given the number of tobiano × tobiano matings, this is an area for more study. Naturally, a homozygous tobiano must have both parents tobiano, and will produce 100 per cent tobiano progeny to a mate of any colour (rule 1, lines 1 and 6, page 13).

Testing program
A tobiano testing program known as blood marker analysis is available in the United States to screen tobiano horses for homozygosity. The test is not a direct test, but uses the weight of evidence of several factors to prove homozygosity.

This can save a breeder many years of test breeding stallions and enable selection decisions to be made both quickly and accurately. Furthermore, once a homozygous stallion has been located it can be crossed with pure-bred stock of other breeds to upgrade existing stock without losing tobiano colour (rule 3, line 3, page 13). Once the parent stock is established as homozygous, all the resulting offspring will be homozygous.

Blood marker analysis is based on the premise that certain colour loci in horses can be closely or loosely linked to certain serum protein loci, the inheritance of which is well known and may be easily traced in the laboratory by analysing blood samples. Chestnut, roan and tobiano loci are part

Chestnut tobiano with ink-spots, Peppy's Princess Charm. This horse is heterozygous tobiano as one parent is the Paint Horse Peppy's Doc Bar (imp.USA), a sabino crop-out Quarter Horse

of a linkage group in Paint Horses. Linkage studies may well be the way to solve difficult issues of coat colour inheritance of horses in the future.

Persons interested in finding out more about tobiano test screening should refer to Bowling (1996) or contact:

Spotted Horse Research Group
Department of Biology
Portland State University
Box 751, Portland OR 97207 USA

Champagne King, an Australian tobiano Standardbred from a coloured Snow Time mare, owned by Rebecca Lund

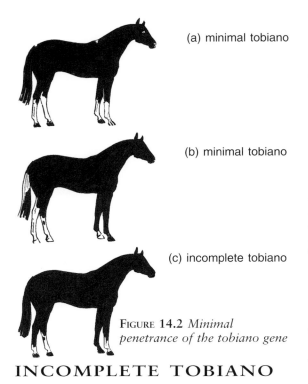

(a) minimal tobiano

(b) minimal tobiano

(c) incomplete tobiano

FIGURE **14.2** *Minimal penetrance of the tobiano gene*

INCOMPLETE TOBIANO

Occasionally an apparent non-tobiano parent that has leg markings, without any other characteristics, produces normal tobiano from a solid mate. The parent is an incomplete tobiano. I know of one with as little white as two hind legs, a Shetland Pony. Mule breeders often use tobiano mares to produce the mule with white stockings, as the donkey is without tobiano and sabino modifiers to contribute to the pattern. Even rarer are reports of tobiano progeny from totally solid parents. Parentage testing has yet to confirm any of these cases.

BREEDS ACCEPTING TOBIANO

No breed has developed exclusively around the tobiano colour, in spite of its ease of production. At one stage in Europe, after the Baroque period, any flashy coloured horse was considered vulgar. If it had not been for Spanish interest, many interesting colours might have died out.

Even so, tobiano was not well known in Spain, so it is likely the colour survived through some of the more primitive and coldblooded breeds. The Shetland has a large number of tobianos which have always been accepted quite favourably, and it is doubtful if any other type of pinto colour exists within the breed. The Australian Stock Horse stud book also accepts the tobiano, as do many Warmblood and Sporthorse stud books. The Paint Horse, a pinto breed originating in the United States, is based on Thoroughbred and Quarter Horse bloodlines. The Pinto Registry, on the other hand, accepts all non-gaited and non-coldblooded horses with the desired markings.

In these breeds, stallions are sometimes advertised on the basis of their coloured foal percentage, the premise being that a high colour production is less risky to mare owners wishing to produce colour. These figures can be quite misleading, however, unless number of foals and colour of the mates are also reported. Mare owners and buyers would do well to make their own investigations with the appropriate stud books to determine the validity of these claims.

Tobiano Standardbreds
There are approximately 150 tobiano Standardbreds remaining in the world, of which the main lines are:
- Snow Fall—mare 1961 (this line is now defunct);
- Deep Snow—mare 1962 (only one mare left in this line);
- Snow Time—stallion 1958 (this line is going strong);
- Elegant—mare 1951 (this line is going strong); and
- Pye's Indian Chief—mare (only three of breeding age remain).

Curiously there is also one splashed white line (through Total Colour—mare 1987) and a cream (palomino) line (through Cream Beauty—mare 1960). There are thought to be only five cream Standardbreds in existence (M. Lund, 1997, personal communication).

SKJEVET

Geurts (1977) reports a particular type of pinto called *skjevet* (pronounced skew-yet) which once occurred in Fjord ponies. (The Standard of Excellence of the Fjord breed makes no mention of white markings. In fact, white markings of any sort in the breed are discouraged). The skjevet marking is an oblique slash down the shoulders; some have white legs, spots on the white and ticking. Chances are that the marking is a fixed pattern of modifiers of the tobiano gene.

15

SABINO

Quick Guide: Sabino

- Sabino is a dominant pattern of white patches which appear to run vertically up the legs and underbelly/neck, accompanied by large ragged splashes, spots and ticking.
- The head has a large blaze and chinspot.
- Sabino occurs in nearly every breed of horse in minimal form as normal white markings.
- Large white sabino markings, sufficient to qualify as a pinto, can occur in any breed.
- In breeds which disallow the registration of such horses, the spontaneous occurrence of full-blown pinto markings is known as crop-out.
- Crop-out sabino occurs quite regularly in some breeds.
- Sabino is frequently confused with overo and roan.

Technically, any horse with a chinspot, white above the midline of the knee or diminishing spear above the hock (with or without a belly patch, no matter how small) is a genetic sabino (pronounced sa-bee-no). Sabino is rarely described because it is frequently confused with overo, or listed as a subtype called 'calico overo'. In the early Australian literature sabinos were known as 'banjo' horses.

Sabino can range from marginal white (as shown on the horse on page 63) through to the classic peaked sabino (where the splashes appear to peak at any/all of the buttocks, hips, ribs, shoulders and neck), to extensive white, such as medicine hat and all-white (sabino-white).

Many show extensive ticking. In extensive white sabinos, the dark spots may also become larger or shift position somewhat with age. Repigmentation, producing spots and speckles much like flea-bites or heads of wheat, is quite common in older sabino-whites. All these variations are possible in the heterozygote, proving sabino to be dominant in nature.

On the other hand, when a sabino foal is produced from apparently solid parents, the foal is described as a 'crop-out', suggesting that sabino is recessive. This is the true crop-out, the individual

Features of the sabino

- A patch (or patches) present on the underside at belly, girth or breast, following the underside of the neck;
- Body white appears to run vertically up the body, terminating in irregular peaks or splashes of diminishing size;
- Chinspot;
- White legs with white hooves and at least one white leg with diminishing spear or ∧ point edge;
- Ticking.

that has normal parents so that its patterned marking comes as a complete surprise. However, we also know that sabino × sabino can produce a solid foal, which could not be possible if sabino is recessive.

I believe that sabino is the controlling mechanism for white markings in all solid horses, and that the sabino pattern is the natural expansion of white seen on the average horse.

For want of anything better, I will advance this theory in Chapter 19 on white markings (page 88).

Lethal defects have never been reported in sabinos in Australia and they can be safely bred to any other pinto pattern. Glass eyes occur quite frequently when the blaze runs near to or into the eye, in particular in the Clydesdale, where sabino is not discriminated against. In fact, the native Scottish mares that were first crossed with the Flemish horse to produce the breed were inclined to be sabino. These mares were so highly prized, in particular any with a spot on the belly, that during the formative years of the Clydesdale breed the colour was positively selected, as it was believed that this would enhance the retention of the breed's foundation characteristics.

Classic black sabino

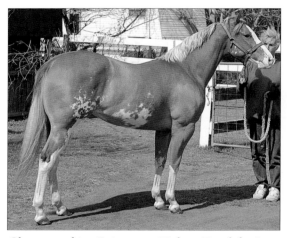

Chestnut sabino Paint mare Holster Touch by Lace

Extensive sabino Clydesdale with repigmentation specks

Chestnut sabino

Rount

The Clydesdale is the breed most frequently associated with sabino, although here it is usually described as 'roan'. No true roan exists in the Clydesdale. Very occasionally one finds a Clydesdale with dark legs, although at least one leg will be white. It is recommended that sabino Clydesdales be bred to a dark-legged Clydesdale to reduce the incidence of excessively white animals, which are more prone to skin cancers and harness chafing.

Sabino is also associated with the Arabian breed, where 'high white', as it is known, is a frequent occurrence, although seldom to the extent exhibited in the Clydesdale. According to some sources, the term *sabino* was Spanish for 'roan'. This roan was, in fact, the colour often described as roan in the Clydesdale and Arabian which we know to be sabino. Other sources state that *sabino* means 'pertaining to the township of Sabino', a town in northern Italy. Common usage worldwide has meant the term 'sabino' now describes a broken colour.

Associated with sabino is speckled ticking or 'roaning', similar to the coon-tailed tick, but without the horizontal banded tail, although some white hairs are usually seen in the tail. Particularly striking is the 'feathered' sabino, so called because the splotches of white resemble small white feathers blown onto the horse. Extensive ticking is why so many sabinos have incorrectly been referred to as 'roan'. Probably 80 per cent of sabinos exhibit this ticking to a minor or greater degree, so that ticking is an excellent indicator of the minimal sabino. Nevertheless, ticking occurs in horses without sabino characteristics and not all sabinos exhibit ticking.

ROUNT

Heavy ticking can create a form of sabino that is subject to fading or 'roaning out'. This is not part of the greying process, or the silvering which occurs in some Appaloosas. Known as 'rount' or 'grizzle' in Europe (after the pigeon of the same name which is white-and-grey flecked), the rount horse is marked with ill-defined 'roan' and white blotches scattered randomly over the coat in such a way that the horse can look both pink and blue, depending on the base colour and the colour of the skin underneath. This subtype is most likely recessive as both parents may be non-ticked. The colour is most commonly seen in the Clydesdale, Criollo and Paint Horse.

Brown sabino Clydesdale. Notice the mouth patch which is ʌ pointed, rather than rectangular as in the overo

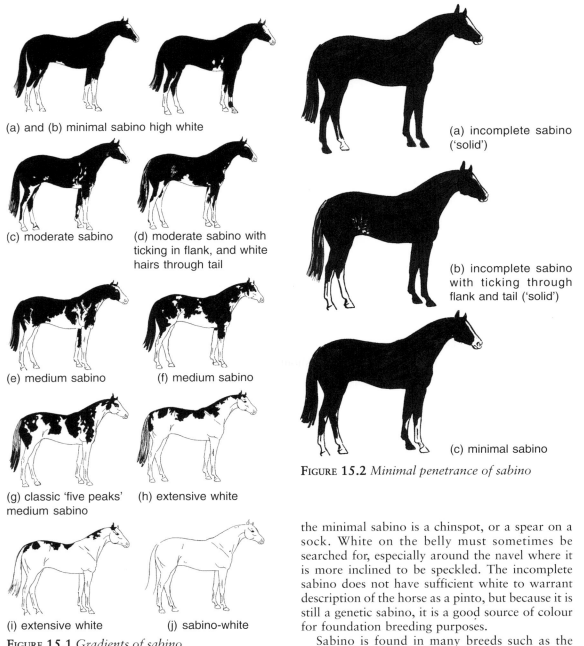

(a) and (b) minimal sabino high white

(c) moderate sabino

(d) moderate sabino with ticking in flank, and white hairs through tail

(e) medium sabino

(f) medium sabino

(g) classic 'five peaks' medium sabino

(h) extensive white

(i) extensive white

(j) sabino-white

FIGURE 15.1 *Gradients of sabino*

(a) incomplete sabino ('solid')

(b) incomplete sabino with ticking through flank and tail ('solid')

(c) minimal sabino

FIGURE 15.2 *Minimal penetrance of sabino*

INCOMPLETE SABINOS

There are many 'solid' horses without excessive white that still carry the sabino factor, such as the horse pictured on page 19. A sabino horse rarely has four dark legs. The most reliable indicator in the minimal sabino is a chinspot, or a spear on a sock. White on the belly must sometimes be searched for, especially around the navel where it is more inclined to be speckled. The incomplete sabino does not have sufficient white to warrant description of the horse as a pinto, but because it is still a genetic sabino, it is a good source of colour for foundation breeding purposes.

Sabino is found in many breeds such as the American Saddlebred, Arabian, Criollo, Hackney, Quarter Horse, Standardbred, Tennessee Walking Horse, Thoroughbred, Welsh Pony, some Warmbloods and Draught breeds, and the lesser known Indian breed, the Kathiawari. The American Paint Horse Association does not separately identify sabino, even though I estimate over 80 per cent of their horses are sabino or sabino combinations.

16

OVERO

Quick Guide: Overo

- Overo is a dominant pattern of white patches that appears to spread horizontally along the ribs, neck and body, leaving the topline and legs still coloured.
- The face has large irregular white.
- An overo must have one overo parent, even if incompletely marked.
- Incomplete overo in one of the parents is the reason for the apparent spontaneous appearance of overo in the Quarter Horse.
- There is no such thing as a true crop-out.
- A homozygous overo foal is born white and dies soon after birth from lethal defects.
- Homozygous overo is always lethal. It is produced from mating of two overos.
- All overos carry the lethal white factor.
- For humane reasons, overo should be bred to a normal solid horse.
- Overo bred to solid gives 50 per cent overo.

No colour pattern has been the subject of as much confusion over its identification and inheritance as the overo (pronounced o-year-o). In many respects the overo is an opposite (or negative) of the tobiano.

Overo is the only pinto pattern that can have all legs dark. In minimal cases, white tends to be located on the side of the neck, sometimes just as a single spot, and along the ribs. It spreads horizontally along the neck and body, appearing on the quarters last of all. When white appears on the neck, colour remains in the throat. In extensive white horses, colour tends to be restricted to the borders, thus 'framing' the horse in colour. Indeed these horses are called 'frame' overos. These borders are the hocks, upper arms, spine between withers and tail, chest, underside of the neck and poll.

Although the white patches sometimes have vertical characteristics, known as lightning or flash marks (commonly a strip of white up the front of the forearm), it is the horizontal expansion of white that is the most reliable feature of the overo.

One of the more striking features is the extensive white on the face. Unlike the white markings of solid horses, these are large and asymmetrical, often taking in the whole face. One side may be quite white, the other with hardly any white at all, like Holster Hi Shadow. These unusual markings have names such as 'apron face', 'bonnet face' or 'bald', which describe the positioning of the white. White which has 'slipped' into the eye will sometimes give a wall eye. One or two wall eyes are relatively common. These are usually referred to as 'blue' eyes by Paint people.

Most overos, in spite of extensive white on the head, retain a large patch of colour over the eyes,

Features of the overo

- Body white tends not to cross the spine except in extensively marked individuals;
- Legs dark up to the knee unless sabino is present;
- Body white is irregular, appearing to spread horizontally;
- Tail full coloured, except in extensively marked individuals;
- Large, irregular white face markings.

Black overo Paint Horse stallion Holster Hi Shadow, both sides, showing flash marks on thigh and forearm

thus keeping a dark eye and protecting the area. One can even find colour restricted to the eyelids, like women's eyeliner. This is a characteristic that could be selectively bred to advantage. Due to the extent of white on the face, many overos suffer from sunburn, allergy and related problems.

THE MEDICINE HAT

Nearly all-white individuals, known as medicine hat overos, are found. In fact they can be completely white with speckles over the skin. These are overo/sabino crosses (sabero) or less commonly tobiano/overo crosses (tobero), or a combination of all three (tovino).

A breed based almost entirely on the medicine hat is the Moroccan Barb. The foundation animals were Hackney, French Coach Horses and Saddlebreds, mostly sabino, but a few were overo or tobiano. The American Spanish Mustang registry (which doesn't allow tobianos as it is believed that tobiano is not a true Spanish marking) produces a huge number of medicine hats.

ORIGIN OF THE OVERO

Overo has not been a colour of European horse breeds and is thought to be a mutation that first occurred in the New World. For quarantine reasons, New World blood has not had an influence on the Australian horse, with the result that overo only appeared in Australia with the importation of American Paint stock in the early 1970s. Australia then

Framed overo Paint Horse stallion C-Notes Playboy (imp.USA) (photo Peta-Anne)

became one giant testing ground for the study of the overo coat pattern. Crossed with the Thoroughbred and other foundation stock with, quite obviously, no overo breeding background, the overo reproduced in typical Mendelian fashion as a simple dominant. Lethal white foals were unheard of until the introduction of overos to this country, and these only occurred in matings of overo parents.

The inheritance of overo, then, was well and truly clear-cut, and I first reported this in the Australian *Hoofs and Horns* magazine in October 1982. Shortly afterwards Australian Pinto groups adopted this as fundamental, recognising both sabino and overo. Paint groups were slow to respond and at the time of writing, sabino is still not officially recognised by American parent breed associations. Overo has largely been thought to be recessive by geneticists in the United States (until Bowling, 1996). This is due to confusion with sabino, which is infrequently recognised as a separate colour pattern in its own right, and is generally not very well understood.

It has been suggested in the United States that there are several subtypes of overo. The Australian experience does not support this, as the subtypes suggested, sabino and splashed white (Chapter 17), have always been present in Australia. For this

reason the sabino and splashed white should never be referred to as overo.

Once a breeder understands the sabino colour pattern, an understanding of all the other broken-coloured patterns falls into place.

Now that it is possible to do blood marker analysis on overo and tobiano, it should be possible by exclusion to identify as sabino those horses not carrying the overo or tobiano blood marker.

LETHAL WHITE OR WHITE FOAL SYNDROME

Overo is inherited as a simple dominant symbolised as O^o for overo and O^+ for non-overo. O^oO^o individuals are born all-white (occasionally with a few spots), with light blue irises and normal pigmented retinas. They are not viable due to defective bowel formation and often have other deformities.

A similar rare genetic disease is reported in man. All overo-white foals die a few hours after birth, so it is more humane to euthanise at once.

This defect, known as 'lethal white' or more correctly 'white foal syndrome', only occurs in the

Medicine hat overo Paint stallion Holster Touch of Hillbilly, with colour remaining only on the ears

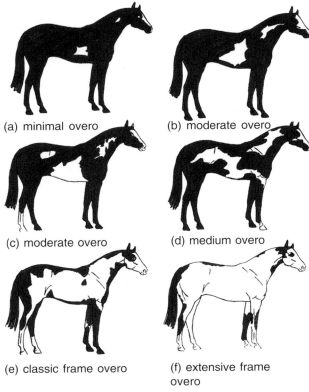

(a) minimal overo

(b) moderate overo

(c) moderate overo

(d) medium overo

(e) classic frame overo

(f) extensive frame overo

FIGURE **16.1** *Gradients of overo*

homozygous form, so that heterozygous (carrier) individuals are sound. The defect is said to be the result of a dominant gene with recessive lethal effect. Both the cells that produce colour in the skin (melanocytes), and the cells that produce the intestine (ganglia cells), originate in the same area of the developing foetus called the neural crest. When melanocytes are absent, as in the all-white foal, so too are the ganglia cells which allow the normal action of passing food through the intestine.

Recently the University of Minnesota Veterinary Genetics Lab has developed a test for Overo Lethal White syndrome (OLWS) in 'carrier' individuals, using unclotted blood. I believe all overos tested will prove to be 'carriers', thus rendering the test obsolete in true overos. This will then become the definitive test to identify doubtful overos and sabino mimics which cannot presently be identified by phenotype alone.

Why have we not heard of a 25 per cent incidence of lethal white, since lethal white should occur in 25 per cent of all overo × overo matings? (rule 4, line 4 page 13.)

The Australian Paint Horse Association hears of very few lethal white foals born per year. Firstly, I would suggest that not many overo × overo matings actually occur. Most are overo × sabino, or even sabino × sabino, described incorrectly. Most overos are bred to non-coloured mates, which is the preferred option.

Secondly, it is suggested, although less likely, that due to their defective nature, some overo-whites may not be sufficiently viable to maintain normal development and would be resorbed or aborted before the breeder was aware of pregnancy.

Finally, there is a 'not in our stud' syndrome that occurs in any breed where a difficult issue needs addressing. The incidence is probably higher than is officially reported.

Are all overo-whites lethal?

According to current knowledge the answer is yes. It has been suggested that if the defect is linked to the overo gene it is possible that some overos are free of the linkage.

As proof of this, we would occasionally get an all-white individual (overo-white) that lives to reproduce; under these circumstances, it would be a 100 per cent overo producer.

Another suggestion is that some O^oO^o individuals carry minimal colour and are not all-white. These could escape the defect, but would still produce 100 per cent overo. However, Paint records have yet to show any overo stallion with sufficient progeny that has sired only overo foals, giving no support to such theories.

Can one avoid breeding a lethal white?

By never breeding overo to overo but always to solid coloured stock, good percentage overo colour production occurs (50 per cent—rule 5, line 5, page 13), but without any possibility of lethal white.

Why not breed overo to tobiano or sabino?

One will certainly achieve a higher percentage of coloured foals, but I would suggest that breeding combination patterns destroys the integrity of the individual patterns. We start getting too many 'mongrel', neither one nor the other, progeny. The more we superimpose various combinations of pied markings in the one horse, the more we lose colour and are left with a mostly white horse.

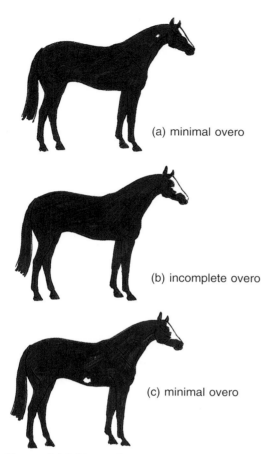

(a) minimal overo

(b) incomplete overo

(c) minimal overo

FIGURE 16.2 *Minimal overo*

The aim of the coloured horse breeder is to breed contrast, not white.

Further, the composite of overo with other pinto patterns leaves a phenotype that could be difficult to identify as carrying overo. In the next generation, if this were unknowingly bred back to overo, another lethal white foal could result. For this reason OLWS testing should become mandatory in colour breeds.

INCOMPLETE OVERO

It is possible for overo markings to be so reduced as to not be recognisable overo. The horse could have an awkward blaze or just one small spot on the neck or forearm, but it would have some white.

It might appear to be solid with blue eyes. This horse would be referred to as solid when in fact it would be an incomplete overo. Such minimal action is recognised to occur in other species as 'dominant with variable penetrance'.

Incomplete overo frequently occurs when one of the parents is a total solid. Breeders report very low overo colour production when total solids are used in Paint Horse breeding programmes.

This leads us to a number of issues. Loud or flashy overo has been reported in some of the early American Paint horses whose sires and dams are registered in the foundation of the American Quarter Horse Association Stud Book. These have AQHA after their names.

Several AQHA horses were registered with excessive white at that time, due to lack of knowledge in the early years, but their pedigrees do not give any indication of this excessive white. Others were listed as having unknown bloodlines. Most 'excessive white' horses would have been sabino, but a few of them would have been minimal overo.

WHAT IS THE CROP-OUT?

Nearly always, the so-called 'crop-out' is, in fact, a sabino which results from normal solid-coloured parents, usually in pure-breeds which by regulation are required to be solid-coloured. There is no occurrence of true overo from true non-overo parents that has been verified by parentage testing in Australia.

The occasional report of solid × solid producing overo would need to be confirmed by parentage testing and OLWS testing. It will be found that at least one of the 'solid' parents is in fact a minimal or incomplete overo.

If overo from solid parents occurred, the trigger would come from an overo in the background of the parents (since the trigger didn't appear in Australia until the importation of overo Paint Horses).

If such cases occurred at all, they would be extremely rare and are more likely to be a case of misidentification of the parents. OLWS testing will show that one of the 'solid' parents is in fact minimal or incomplete overo.

17

SPLASHED WHITE

> ## Quick Guide: Splashed white
>
> - Splashed white is a dominant pattern where white appears horizontally across the bottom half of the body and tail.
> - The face is bald with blue eyes.
> - Deafness is an associated characteristic.
> - One parent will be splashed white even in apparent crop-outs.
> - Splashed white is best bred to solid for 50 per cent splashed.
> - Splashed white is thought to be non-viable in homozygous form, but does not result in lethal foals like overo crosses.

Imagine swimming your horse in a sea of white paint so that the top of its body stays dry while the rest is splashed in paint. This is the rare splashed white, quite often simply referred to as 'splashed'.

Features of the splashed white

- Body dark on top half, white on lower half;
- Bald white head;
- White or bottom half white tail;
- Two wall eyes.

First impression of the splashed white is of a sabino, but the edges of the colour are not as indistinct or mottled as in the true sabino, rather they are square-cut. There is no associated ticking either. In medium marked horses, white runs across the body horizontally, over the belly and underside of the neck, but with the occasional peak of white like splashes of a wave. Splashed white horses with extreme white have the last remnants of pigment round the ears and eyes and on the croup. They may have one or two white ears, or both ears dark. The legs are always white, with distinctive square-cut top.

Some splashed whites also share the sabino gene which makes identification difficult. Splashed white without sabino has a clean-cut look with squared edges, whereas the sabino mix has speckles and a peaked appearance in the body pattern. All splashed whites clinically tested to date in Australia, are deaf.

Sometimes, even the owner is unaware of this feature until it is pointed out, because the horse performs no differently and has a calm temperament. However not all deaf pinto horses are splashed whites, as an occasional overo with two blue eyes will also be deaf.

Unlike splashed whites, deaf blue-eyed overos tend to go blind with age. Since quite a few splashed white lines are now being identified in the USA, there appears to be a tendency to claim that any overo with two blue eyes is a splashed white. Given that a few bald-faced overos are deaf anyway, it may be difficult to separate the two and it may be more likely that some are combinations. Splashed white is one of the few colours in the horse where a single gene may have other (pleiotropic) effects. A similar gene occurs in mice where part of the middle ear is absent.

Testing on the Australian Millard line of splashed white horses (page 81) shows a connection between the splashed white gene and human syndromes such as spina bifida and Waardenburg's syndrome.

Splashed white has been widely reported in the Finnish Horse (where it is referred to as Finnish Paint), in the Miniature Horse, Welsh Pony and Quarter Horse. One breed, the Abaco Horse of the Bahamas, is thought to be exclusively splashed white or solid. The Australian Thoroughbred stallion, Whata Picture (Grey Mop × Hidden Star, 1970), was a splashed white mutation registered as 'grey or bay' and subsequently went grey. He was deaf and sired a few splashed white progeny before being gelded. It is believed this line is now defunct.

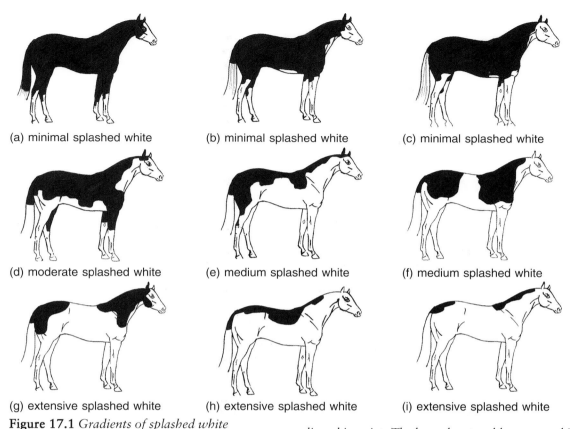

(a) minimal splashed white

(b) minimal splashed white

(c) minimal splashed white

(d) moderate splashed white

(e) medium splashed white

(f) medium splashed white

(g) extensive splashed white

(h) extensive splashed white

(i) extensive splashed white

Figure 17.1 *Gradients of splashed white*

Because splashed white occurs in such isolated examples throughout the world, its first occurrence in any breed is probably through mutation. Splashed white is unheard of in Welsh Ponies in Australia.

None of the non-splashed white progeny in Australia have exhibited a wall eye, nor have non-splashed white descendants ever produced splashed white themselves. Observations of the Millard line and others reveals transmission is by simple dominance (*Spl*^{S}). Millard has bred a splashed white mare with her splashed white sire on three occasions and in each case the mare has aborted at three months, suggesting splashed white is lethal in double dose.

INCOMPLETE SPLASHED WHITE

Incomplete splashed white has been observed with as little as four white pasterns and without the white-dipped tail. In every case of incomplete splashed white to date, the face is bald as if the mouth is dipped in paint. The horse has two blue eyes and is deaf. Such a colour is usually seen in Miniature Horses, breeding-stock Paints, and more rarely in the Quarter Horse, where they tend to be identified as solid. Incomplete splashed white parentage may explain why, in the Finnish Paint at least, splashed white has been thought to be recessive. No reports of deafness in this breed have been published.

THE MILLARD LINE

The origin of the Millard horses is unknown, although it is accepted that they do not descend from imported American Paint stock. Leanne Millard says of her particular line of splashed whites:

In a lot of cases the owner does not know that the horse is deaf as they are very alert and act no differently to a horse that can hear. Their ears are always moving. I have observed extreme 'braininess', super smell and eyesight, and an almost unflappable temperament. They are also very sensitive in the hoof when shoeing and I believe

81

TOP: *Splashed white Paint Horse racing stallion Gambling Man.* BOTTOM: *Bay splashed white Paint Horse, Hot Gossip.* LEFT: *Incomplete splashed white Miniature Horse foal Tiny Toy Geminizer; sire: 4 Go Fullers Equalizer, pictured on page 119 (photo M. Bennett)*

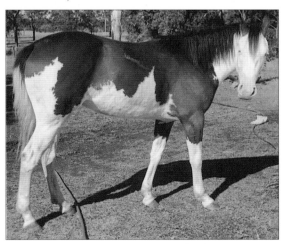

they feel vibrations through the ground. One can fire a gun alongside a sleeping splashed white and the horse will not hear, yet you can drop a heavy brick and the horse will wake up. The horses also have a narrower set of the ears and very broad fore-

heads. The blue in the eyes is a cloudy blue-grey, making the eye slightly different than the blue eye of the sabino and overo; these differences are readily apparent when seeing them side by side with normal Paint Horses.

Breeders are faced with the dilemma that to preserve this colour, there are moral responsibilities. Ethically, there would be a duty of disclosure to an unsuspecting buyer if the horse is deaf, along with the possible difficulties of which the new owner would need to be made aware.

One cannot assume that because a horse is deaf the horse need live a less than useful life. Horses follow body language and way too much credit is given to the use of voice in communicating with them. Remember Clever Hans, the horse that could 'count' because he read the answers from his owner's body language? Stuntwork with horses at liberty has even been done for commercials by humans signalling from a helicopter.

Temperament is one of the hardest characteristics to fix in horse breeding.

'Ideal' temperament may be a multiplicity of heterozygous factors anyway—so little is known about its inheritance—and so many other non-heritable factors must be taken into consideration.

The responsibility of the horse breeder in selecting for temperament, even in the racehorse where temperament is often overlooked for the almighty dollar, cannot be underestimated. All reputable breeders spend a lifetime preserving and improving the temperament of their horses. They know it is the hardest thing to keep in a herd and the easiest characteristic to lose. In fact, this is the major reason why some breeders come and go, while others establish a reputation and remain reputable for years.

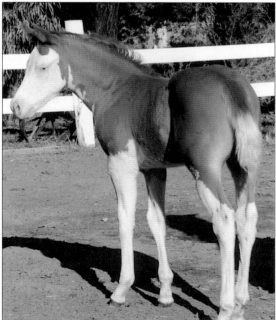

TOP: *Extensive splashed white chestnut Paint Horse stallion Keno's Dynamite (photo D. Shugart)*
BOTTOM: *Chestnut minimal splashed white Paint Horse foal*

83

18

COMPOSITE BROKEN COLOURS

> **Quick Guide: Composite broken colours**
>
> - There are four patterns in pinto-coloured horses: tobiano, sabino, overo and splashed white.
> - All these patterns are dominant.
> - The medicine hat is always sabino, but may occur in combination with tobiano, overo or even splashed white.
> - Composites are usually high percentage colour producers.
> - Combination matings occur frequently and are to be discouraged as they too often lead to a mostly white horse of limited economic value.
> - Since it is difficult to determine the genotype of such horses they should be bred to a normal solid, especially if overo is suspected.
> - Pinto can coexist with Appaloosa spotting. Such crosses are not recognised by most breeds so usually reflect poor breeding.

The four forms of pinto can exist alongside one another as the genes for each type operate on separate loci. We have To^T (Tobiano), O^O (Overo), Sb^S (Sabino) and Spl^S (Splashed white).Ordinary solid-coloured horses will contain To^+, O^+, Sb^+ and Spl^+ in their genotype ($To^+To^+O^+O^+Sb^+Sb^+Spl^+Spl^+$) as solid colour is the wild expression, but we do not include these in solid × solid colour calculations, as each horse would be the same and it becomes irrelevant. When we have a horse that has more than one type of pinto pattern, we see evidence of each exhibited in the appearance of the horse.

IDENTIFYING DIFFICULT PHENOTYPES

The most confusing issue for Paint Horse breeders is the regular occurence of sabino amongst the tobiano and overo genotypes. In particular, sabino can mimic overo. This frequently remains unrecognised but alters foal options, particularly in regard to lethal white.

Further confusion can occur in combinations that have minimal characteristics of one colour merging with loud characteristics of another. Often, the only

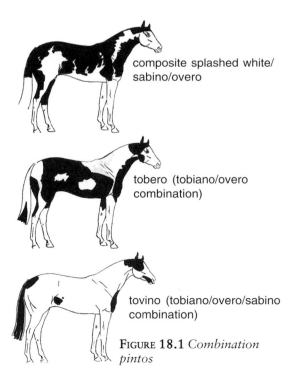

composite splashed white/ sabino/overo

tobero (tobiano/overo combination)

tovino (tobiano/overo/sabino combination)

FIGURE **18**.1 *Combination pintos*

way to ascertain the full genotype of a certain horse is to breed it to a solid colour several times and even this may not reveal sufficient information.

Combinations of splashed white and all the other pinto colours can be found, but are less common. Splashed white is most frequently found in combination with sabino. According to Millard (1996, personal communication), the splashed white/sabino mix gives the peaked body edge rather than the straight square-cut look typical of the splashed white, and plenty of ticking. The bay pictured on page 82 could be a sabino combination.

OTHER COMBINATIONS

Occasionally pinto and spotting can coexist, producing the 'pintaloosa'.

Multi-combinations are usually indicative of unplanned or poorly devised breeding programs, which have made insufficient use of quality parentage or pure-bred upgrading programs. Having said that, in the Miniature Horse colour combinations are planned quite regularly so as to give herds of multi-colours, which are interesting to look at and are attractive to buyers.

Experienced colour breeders will select for 50/50 contrast to give the desired impact and individuality the market place prefers. Mostly white horses tend to be more difficult to sell. Breeders

---

Examples of composite pintos

Tobero* = tobiano + overo
$$To^T\_O^OO^+Sb^+Sb^+$$
Tobino = tobiano + sabino $To^T\_O^+O^+Sb^S\_$
Sabero = sabino + overo
$$To^+To^+O^OO^+Sb^S\_$$
Tovino = tobiano + overo + sabino
$$To^T\_O^OO^+Sb^S\_$$

Footnote to table

*Tobero is also known as tovero.

Table 18.1 Identifying the four pinto patterns				
	TOBIANO	OVERO	SABINO	SPLASHED WHITE
HEAD	Dark, eyes dark or blue	Off-centre blaze, apron or bald, eyes dark or blue	White chin or underjaw, eyes dark or blue	Bald with blue eyes
NECK	White from crest down	White zigzag along centre, throat dark	White throat & underside, vertical peaks	White underside, squared edges
BODY	Vertical white, shielded patches of colour	Irregular, patches of white especially on ribs	Vertical white splashes & peaks, ticking, belly patches	Dark top half, white bottom half, square-cut look
LEGS	White with chestnut & ermine spots	Dark	White, spear-edged	White, square-topped
TAIL	Dark or white or bi-coloured	Dark	Dark or white-streaked	Dark top, white bottom

Footnote to table

These descriptions are not definitive. As not all horses exhibit all features, or may mimic others, identification must be based on the sum total of identifying characteristics.

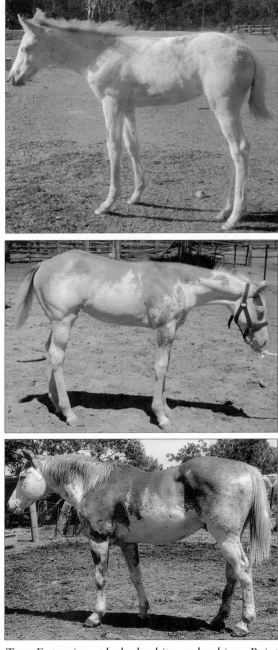

TOP: *Sabero Paint Horse stallion Gambling Rudytooty.* CENTRE: *Tobino or tovino Paint Horse stallion Gambling Prospect.* BOTTOM: *Chestnut tobino Rondoro Leilani.*

TOP: *Extensive splashed white and sabino, Paint Horse CLM's Morse Code by Bald Eagle.* CENTRE: *Yellow dun splashed white and sabino CLM's Dunup Lovely sired by Bald Eagle.* BOTTOM: *Paint Horse stallion Bald Eagle, prolific sire of the Millard line of splashed white horses, with sabino combination almost obliterating the splashed white pattern*

(a) straight overo (no evidence of sabino)

(b) straight overo—no white on throat, apron crosses cheek and meets white of neck above the throat

(c) straight sabino—chinspot, speckles on throat, no overo characteristics

(d) straight sabino—white under neck and on throat, speckled edges, no overo characteristics

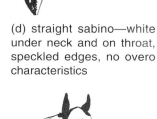

(e) sabero—sabino/overo combination

(f) sabero—sabino/overo combination (medicine hat)

FIGURE **18.2** *Identifying sabino, overo and the combination (sabero) by head and neck markings.*

FIGURE **18.3** *Splashed white/sabino combinations: pointed look; edges are also speckled*

will choose the base colours of black, brown, bay and chestnut; if some other foundation colour such as grey or roan is used, the integrity of the desired colour pattern could be lost.

In a wise and methodical breeding program colour combinations will not be intermixed.

Upgrading will be maintained by the thoughtful introduction of pure-bred blood of a well-regarded, compatible breed, so as to retain the performance characteristics which that breed has to offer.

Black tobiano and dark spotted blanket Miniature Horse stallion Tiny Toy Holy Smoke

87

19

WHITE MARKINGS

Quick Guide: White Markings

- White markings are frowned upon in some breeds, and highly desired in others.
- In most breeds, white markings do not go above an artificial line determined by breed regulations. These horses are known as solids.
- White markings are the result of the dominant sabino gene.
- The amount of white is determined by modifying genes which may be fixed by selective breeding to be minimal or extensive, or in certain positions.
- Horses without white at all are produced by the action of another factor, a gene for 'no white' or total solid.
- In some breeds the majority of horses are total solid.

Many horse breeders and buyers share an enthusiasm for plenty of 'chrome' (loud white markings) on solid horses, as evidenced at any horse show. Only the hack ring seems to keep the tradition of conservatism with dark, subdued colours.

Although flashy, in general white markings are less practical than whole colours and in certain climates are to be avoided due to problems such as greasy heel, rain scald, sunburn, allergy and chafing. White hooves, an extension of pink skin, are notorious for being weaker than black hooves, but this should be considered in conjunction with the breed and foot type. In many breeds and terrains the white hoof is just as durable as its black counterpart, but in the Thoroughbred in particular, which has a tendency towards thin walls and a shelly foot, trouble which arises with frequent plating for racing is magnified when the hoof is white. Consequently in breeds which have a preponderance of Thoroughbred blood, such as the Australian Stock Horse, flashy white is usually avoided. Indeed the Australian Stock Horse is highly regarded for its enduring hooves.

In some locations a 'softer' white hoof can actually help guard against splitting due to the chalkiness which allows smoother wear with less cracking because the hoof is less brittle. White hair itself is of coarser texture than the corresponding surrounding base colour such that it is often possible to differentiate white from dark hairs by touch. Consequently, show enthusiasts will clip out white hair to present a cleaner and more refined look.

WHAT DO WE KNOW ABOUT THE PRESENCE OF WHITE HAIRS?

Recapping, colour genes in the horse create the base colours of black, brown, bay and chestnut, while genes at other loci can either dilute hair colour or create white hairs. Whenever we get pink skin, we automatically get white hairs in the form of pinto, spotting, or face and leg markings.

In the case of white markings, we know that the extent of white is controlled by modifying genes, as yet unidentified, such that these patterns may become 'fixed' in certain areas of the body and be selectively bred within certain bloodlines.

Curiously, identical twins have rarely been reported in horses so research has been limited to other species. In dogs, it is noted that identical pups do not necessarily have identical white markings. Recent work with embryo-splitting techniques in horses has allowed an identical embryo to be placed in a recipient mare, and proven that when it comes to white

Face markings

0. No white
1. Star—white above the eye line
2. Strip or stripe—area between the eye line and above the nostrils which is not wider than the bridge of the nose
3. Snip—white below the top of the nostrils
4. Blaze—a combination of all three, sometimes wider than the bridge of the nose
5. Chinspot—white on lower lip or chin
6. Bald—white which includes both eyes and nostrils

Star and snip would be recorded as 1 and 3, while star, snip and strip would be recorded as 1, 2, and 3.

markings, other mechanisms in addition to heredity are at work influencing the nature and extent of white.

Woolf (1989), following extensive studies in the American Arabian Horse, established a heritability estimate for white facial markings at 68 per cent. This means that 68 per cent of the cause of white markings is due to heredity, the rest is a result of non-genetic factors.

It is known that white markings occur more often on the hind legs than on the forelegs, more often on the left than the right, and on the forehead rather than on the nose. White low on the face tends to have white above it. Why this is so is not known. White markings on the face tend to centre around three sites: the middle of the forehead (star), bridge of the nose (strip) and middle of the nose (snip), with progressive spreading from each site until a blaze is formed. Face markings may also be broken.

We know that for the same number of modifying genes for white markings, a bay will have less white than will a chestnut, and black will have less white again. Homozygous bay is thought to have less white than the heterozygote. Statistical studies also show that males are slightly more marked than females. There also appears to be a high correlation between white socks and white facial markings, although these may be inherited separately.

The size and placement of white depends first on the number of modifying genes present which have an additive effect. In general, this means that the

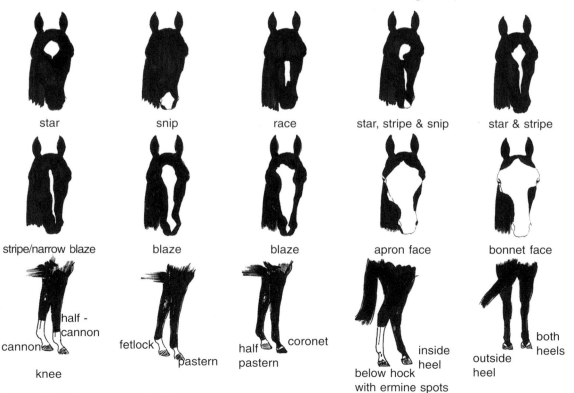

FIGURE 19.1 *Description of white markings*

Badger-faced sabino Clydesdale

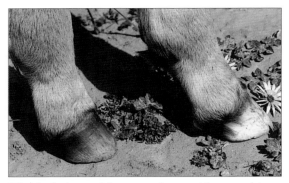

The foal pictured here was born with one white hind foot, but without any white on the leg itself, indicating the genotype N^nN^n. Within two weeks the hoof was growing down black, as the coronary band dictates the colour of the hoof. Unless identified at birth, this foal would be mistakenly thought of as a total solid (N^+_)

amount of white will increase over several generations if selection against it does not occur. Nature tends to select against white in wild herds. Indeed the most primitive breeds rarely exhibit any white. There is also no evidence to suggest that homozygosity for modifiers will increase the amount of white present in a horse, rather it is the sum total of modifiers that counts. A simple numeric recording system for white markings for registration purposes is given here. (It would make life easier for breeders if breed societies adopted a uniform approach.) Information should be derived from good photographs in support of all written applications.

WHERE DO WHITE MARKINGS END, AND SABINO MARKINGS BEGIN?

The answer is not clear. The star and square-cut socks of ordinary horses may be inherited separately from the sabino pattern, but if so would be closely allied to it. Essentially, the chinspot gene *is* the sabino gene. Sabino can occur without the blaze, which gives a 'reverse' or badger face. Occasionally a sabino marking occurs along the front of the hock or knee and does not join onto a sock.

We also get families and some breeds which regularly produce no white at all. I believe there is a locus for no white (N^+) which is dominant over normal white markings (N^n). This means for no white or total solid to occur, one parent must be without white. There could be a separate mechanism for both head and legs, but here we will include them together. Total solid bred to total solid will give total solid 75 per cent of the time (rule 4, line 4, page 13), unless one of the parents is homozygous (rule 2, line 2, page 13), when total solids result 100 per cent of the time.

Leg markings

0. No white
1. Coronet—white marking up to 2.5 cm (1") above the coronary band
2. Pastern—white marking to the bottom of the fetlock joint
3. Fetlock—white marking to the top of the fetlock joint
4. Sock—white marking extending to the midpoint of the cannon
5. Stocking—white marking extending to the excessive white line
6. High white—white extending beyond the line for excessive white

A leg with a partial stocking, say on one side, is still classed as a stocking, or a white heel with partial white hoof is still classed as 1.

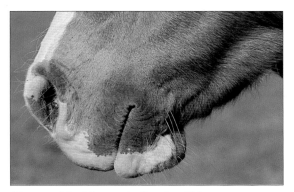

Inheritance of sabino

$N^+\_Sb^S\_$ Total solid horse; no white even though sabino (Sb^S) in genotype.

$N^+\_Sb^+Sb^+$ Total solid horse; no white.

$N^nN^nSb^S\_$ Sabino horse; may be sabino-white or medicine hat, ordinary sabino or high white that does not qualify as pinto, depending on modifiers.

$N^nN^nSb^+Sb^+$ Solid horse; ordinary white, sometimes only a few white hairs on the forehead or coronary band, less often four white socks and blaze (no chinspot, spears on stockings or underbelly markings).

Horse with chinspot indicating Sb^S *present*

We must be aware that where a horse has the genotype N^nN^n, which will permit white markings to occur, the extent of the white would depend entirely on the modifying genes mentioned above, and there are probably many of these. It is also possible, but unusual, that an N^nN^n individual may have no modifying genes at all, so will still have no white markings. (In this case, it is likely that the horse would be considered to be the result of $N^+\_$, when in fact it would be N^nN^n.)

EXCESSIVE WHITE RULE

In breeds which have colour restrictions, white is not permitted:

- above a line around each leg at the centre of the knees and hocks, unless as a diminishing spear;
- behind a line running from the corner of each ear to the corner of each side of the mouth; and
- on the lower lip behind a line running from one corner of the mouth to the other.

Geldings and spayed mares are often permitted greater flexibility in regard to acceptance for registration. With the Quarter Horse, any animal excluded by the excessive white rule is automatically acceptable for colour registration with the Paint Horse Association. In the latter breed, horses with insufficient white may be classed as breeding stock horses, although no distinction between true solids and incompletely marked horses is made. Every attempt should be made to correct this anomaly for the benefit of breeders, in particular, for avoidance of possible lethal white. The following terms have been used in this book to describe the extent of white in a pinto horse:

- **Incomplete**: where tobiano, overo, sabino or splashed white pattern gene occurs to such a limited extent as to leave the horse unrecognisable as a pinto. White does not reach the 'excessive white line' to enable registration to occur and the horse is generally incorrectly regarded as solid.
- **Minimal**: borderline, sufficient white to reach the excessive white line and to qualify for registration.
- **Medium**: approximately equal proportions of white and colour.
- **Extensive**: considerably more white than colour.
- **Medicine hat**: colour only on the head.
- **All-white**: pinto so extensively marked as to appear all-white.

Since incomplete tobiano, overo and splashed white are uncommon, white markings on the legs and face

Without chinspot (Sb$^+$Sb$^+$) showing 'ordinary' white or blaze

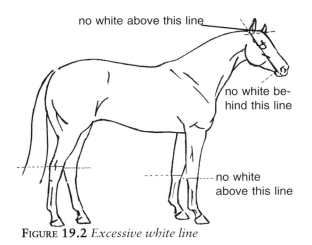

no white above this line

no white behind this line

no white above this line

FIGURE 19.2 *Excessive white line*

of ordinary horses may be regarded as under the control of the sabino (Sb) locus. N^+_ acts as an inhibitor to the expression of white, while N^nN^n allows it. In the presence of Sb^s sabino will occur, while in the presence of Sb^+Sb^+ white will stay below the excessive white line. The N series is the factor behind the apparent recessive nature of sabino. The above table can explain the crop-out appearance of sabino from solid parents. Also, it can explain the appearance of ordinary solid progeny from sabino parents ($N^nN^nSb^sSb^+ \times N^nN^nSb^sSb^+$) (rule 4, line 4, page 13).

Sabino-white probably occurs in both heterozygotes and homozygotes, although I have not investigated this. Two sabinos bred together never produce a total solid or no-white (N^+_) foal. A homozygous N^+N^+ (no white) can never produce a foal with white markings (rule 3, line 3, page 13), although tobiano and overo* are still possible as neither is inhibited by N^+_. I have hypothesised the table at right to explain the interrelationships of white markings with tobiano and overo.

WHAT IS A CROP-OUT?

In reality, there is no such thing as a true crop-out from total solid parents. With the possible exception of sabino, one of the parents will be incomplete, showing white below the line, or alternatively, minimally marked.

TO SUMMARISE

White markings are inhibited by whole colour (N^+). Two pairs of recessives, N^nN^n and Sb^+Sb^+, are re-

Interrelationship between tobiano, overo and white markings

N^+_$O^+O^+To^+To^+$	Solid horse; no white anywhere
$N^nN^nO^+O^+To^+To^+$	Solid horse; ordinary white.
N^+_$O^+O^+To^T$_	Tobiano with solid face.
$N^nN^nO^+O^+To^T$_	Tobiano; ordinary white on face.
N^+_$O^OO^+To^+To^+$	Overo; irregular white on face; no white on legs except from overo modifiers.
$N^nN^nO^OO^+To^+To^+$	Overo; irregular white on face, includes medicine hat; ordinary white on legs.
N^+_O^OO^O_ _	Overo-white—lethal white syndrome.
$N^nN^nO^OO^O$_ _	Overo-white—lethal white syndrome.

All the pinto patterns are dominant, but sabino is the only one that is inhibited, or masked, by the N series which controls the presence or absence of white markings in ordinary solid horses.

*Footnote to table

There is a loose correlation between the presence of minimal sabino and overo. Some have suggested that a threshold level of sabino modifiers must be present before a certain level of expression of overo can occur. The two colours coexist in a large percentage of Paint Horses, although this fact is not well recognised. Most likely this is because of the lack of distinction between sabino and overo in breeding programs.

quired to keep the white limited to 'below the line'. Because this is the norm in most breeds, most matings will never produce sabino. Although the gene for sabino is dominant, some horses carrying the gene will not be excessive whites due to an inadequate number of modifying genes. When bred to another horse that passes on a sufficient number of modifiers, the effect is additive, thus creating the sabino.

White markings, including sabino, are determined by a complex interrelated genetic system as well as unidentified non-genetic factors. Because of high heritability for white markings and sabino, breeders can select for subtypes in which there is no white, minimal white or extensive white.

20

WHITE HORSES

Quick Guide: White Horses

- All-white horses with pink skin and dark eyes, as well as medicine hats, have been recorded in most breeds from time to time.
- The pseudo-albino is not a true white horse, rather it is off-white.
- Grey horses usually go white but they have dark skin.
- White horses may be the result of extensive numbers of modifying genes for Appaloosa, pinto or combinations of these.
- Spontaneous white or crop-out may be explained by the action of the sabino gene.
- Rare white horses are thought to be the result of a dominant white gene (W). No homozygous white horse has been found.
- Dominant white is most likely explained by sabino-white.

White Clydesdale foal, 1933

True white horses (dominant white, pink skin, normal eye colour) are extremely rare. There are, however, many mechanisms that can produce a white-coloured horse, among them grey, which whitens out with age, and can produce early whitening. These horses have a dark hide except where white markings occur. There is the well-known case of MS Czarthan, a white Arabian with dark skin and dark eyes, foaled in the United States in 1967. Both his parents were grey. Investigation revealed he was a grey that had undergone aberrant rapid colour progression before birth, being born in the advanced adult shade of grey, not the usual foal coat. He sired greys.

Cremello and perlino are often thought to be white, but are in fact off-white. In some parts of the world they are called blue-eyed creams or cremes, or mistakenly known as albinos. White horses have been documented in many breeds, including the American Shetland, Appaloosa, Arabian, Brabant, Clydesdale, Gelderland, Paint, Shire, Thoroughbred and Warmblood. Not all of these are from the same genetic source.

A white Appaloosa is a few-spot leopard. A white Paint is a sabino-white or overo/sabino combination. A few also prove to be composite tobianos, or splashed white. Such white horses have minor remnants of base colour as foals which disappear with age. Others will have small amounts remaining, especially around the ears, or through the mane and tail. Repigmentation with mottled skin occurs with age.

An example of the difficulty researchers have with investigating stud book data is that all-white Paint Horses are often recorded as solid, and placed in the Breeding Stock registry!

Sabino-white filly Adina, both parents total solid

SABINO-WHITE

Most all-white horses, throughout the world, are sabino-whites (Sb^s_), which may crop-out from ordinary coloured parents as explained in the chapters on sabino and white markings. White foals in some breeds are relatively uncommon; when they appear they are thought of as crop-outs and known as 'spontaneous white'. Some breeds had large numbers of white horses in their foundation studbooks, such as the Tennessee Walking Horse, or in their foundation bloodlines, such as the Clydesdale and Welsh. In others such as the Arabian, white foals have been recorded quite rarely. More recently white Thoroughbred foals have been regularly reported in the media as their occurrence is still something of a novelty. Some of these white horses produce white foals themselves, although none have produced 100 per cent white. In fact it seems that even 50 per cent white is uncommon, casting doubt that any of these foals could be mutant dominant whites. Spontaneous white is well explained by the sabino factor and such horses should be registered as sabino-white. Their progeny exhibit the full spectrum of white markings from minimal white to high white and classic sabino pinto markings.

Bill Andrew, a very experienced Clydesdale man, remembers as a schoolboy seeing many pure white Clydesdales in Scotland. 'It was not a high incidence, but I would say one in 50. You have to remember at that time there were thousands of Clydesdales working all over Scotland.'

White Arabians, reported as greys with pink skin and blue eyes, or with one blue/one normal eye, were noted over 150 years ago. These were no doubt sabino-whites, for no cremello has one light/one dark eye, and the dilution mechanism C^{cr} as we understand it does not exist in the Arabian. Because new genes are so rarely created (mutation), only recombinations of existing genes can occur in a closed breed like the Arabian. In time we can expect to see the recurrence of white Arabians, as is currently being demonstrated in the Thoroughbred.

The sabino-white has dark brown or dark blue, almost black, eyes. Some have one of each. Surprisingly, although sabinos are sometimes seen with a blue eye, most often in the Clydesdale, it is not as common to see a sabino-white with a blue eye. An interesting question that researchers could look into is why some breeds that numerically have many classic and extensive sabinos, such as the Clydesdale, have a smaller incidence of all-white horses. It seems that the effect of selection on modifying genes plays a great role in 'locking in' the white to specific patterns or variations within breeds.

WHITE FOAL SYNDROME

This is the overo-white foal syndrome as described in Chapter 16. Lethal white occurs in foals which have overo breeding in both parents. Because of the malformed intestine, none survive. It is recommended that overo always be bred to solid to eliminate the risk of overo-white production. Hultgren (1982) reported that the examination of eight overo-white foals revealed blue irises and normal retinas.

Rarely, lethal white is reported in non-overo matings of horses with 'blue eyes'. This is not true white foal syndrome, rather the result of other isolated mechanisms unrelated to overo. Some breeders of pinto horses will only breed a blue-eyed tobiano or overo to a solid, normal-eyed horse, fearing the cross to pinto will produce lethal white. Many breeders hold that the key to understanding the different white mechanisms is closely allied to understanding eye colour. Straight sabino × sabino and tobiano × tobiano matings never produce lethal white.

DOMINANT WHITE

This is the rare true white. True white horses are documented to be the result of a dominant gene W^W which is epistatic to all other colours. They are all white with pink skin and sometimes dark speckles around the genitalia, or elsewhere, which can appear as the horse matures, often around late yearling. The eye colour is normal. They are born white and stay white for life. Homozygotes ($W^W W^W$) are unknown. The mating of two whites results in a ratio of two white foals to one non-white (although some breeders dispute this), which is not in accordance with the laws of Mendelian inheritance. Evidently the $W^W W^W$ embryo is not viable and pregnancy either does not occur or is not maintained, as occurs with roan × roan crosses (see page 62). The incidence of abnormalities in the foals is reported to be no greater than in normal breeding programs.

The most famous white horses of all are those raised from Morgan ancestry on the White Horse

Ranch in Nebraska, in the USA. All are descended from a stallion called Old King foaled in 1906. This bloodline was originally incorporated into a registry called the American Albino Association. Cremellos and perlinos were also accepted, which led to some confusion. Eventually the registry updated its name and its regulations, so that now the true whites are divided from the double-dilutes into a White section and a Creme section. Some composites, with glass eyes, also occur.

Dominant white does not exist in Australia, and to my knowledge all examples of dominant white referred to in the scientific literature could just as easily be explained by the sabino-white mechanism.

DEFECTIVE WHITE

From time to time, reports come in of white horses which don't fit any of the criteria just described. They are thought to be the result of mutation or a genetic stress response. Some which survive subsequently prove to have other defects such as deafness and sterility. Others are healthy themselves but when used for breeding produce a high ratio of lethal deformities, such as contracted tendons, incomplete or absent organ formation and neurological disorders. Mares carrying defective white foals may have a prolonged or difficult birth.

Due to expense and disappointment, and because these horses tend to be isolated examples, little research as to the cause of defective white and its

Dominant white, dark eyes and speckled scrotum

heredity has been carried out. Similar syndromes have been reported in other species including Poll Hereford cattle, dogs, cats, mice and guinea pigs, where the inheritance in most cases is known to be recessive. Equine cases leave many questions unanswered, such as why a parent can be perfectly normal when progeny are not. Speculation also surrounds the colour of the mate. Can we get more defective white horses from chestnut mates (E^eE^e) than say, mates of black, brown and bay colours ($E^+\_$)?

Wherever I travel, breeders speak to me of white-born foals which are not lethal overos. Some die soon after birth. A recent case was of a white-born foal with pink skin and yellow eyes. The foal was weak and died before standing up. Like UFOs, owners seldom mention them in case of stigma and the cause of death is rarely investigated. One thing is certain, the number of unreported white foals is higher than is generally suspected.

COMPOSITE WHITES

All the combinations of white horses listed above could, in theory, exist in the one animal. With the exception of lethal white, all these animals could live to maturity and their appearance would give no indication as to which genes were coexisting. All the pinto/spotted combinations could occur masked by white. There would be no end to the colour possibilities in the progeny of such a white horse.

CASE STUDY I: WHITE THOROUGHBREDS

All grey Thoroughbred horses trace through The Tetrarch to a homozygous mare, foaled in 1789 and receiving both her G^G alleles from her double ancestor, the desertbred Alcock Arabian, foaled in 1700, about 30 horse generations ago. From time to time, white Thoroughbred horses are born which have no grey parents and are not grey. These striking spontaneous white Thoroughbreds to date are all sabino-whites. The first documented white Thoroughbred was the filly Woher born in Germany in 1925. Recent white Thoroughbreds include:

White Beauty 1963 filly, by Ky Colonel from Filly o' Mine. Dark blue, almost black eyes. Born in the United States, raced with some success, retired to stud in 1968. Also by Ky Colonel, and born in the same year, was a white colt with chestnut ears and

a few chestnut spots, War Colours. He died before leaving any get. Of six live foals White Beauty produced, a 1975 filly was white with a few irregular patches (sabino-white), two were sabino, the other three were grey, bay and chestnut. White Beauty died in 1979 foaling another white foal which died. White Beauty had a white granddaughter, Precious Beauty, whose third foal was also white.

Glacial 1966 filly, born in Australia. Some colour in the mane and tail which later faded, one dark eyelid and one pink. By Grey Marwin (grey) from Milady Fair which was an extensively marked bay sabino, exactly like a Clydesdale. Milady Fair 'has never had a normal foal' according to registrar G.W. Lilly, 1972. Of Milady Fair's ten foals, two others are of interest:

- Unnamed—1970 colt, white with bay through the coat, by Istanbul (brown).
- Miasmic—1971 colt, white with chestnut ears and chestnut patches through the coat, by Istanbul.

Of Glacial's eight progeny, two are of interest:

- Khaleben—1972 colt, registered as white-bay in the stud book (bay on head, shoulders and flank), by the brown Khalif (by Istanbul).
  From Surilya, Khaleben sired a sabino colt in 1982. From Cluther, he sired the sabino filly Tetrarch's Lady, and twin white fillies which died at birth. From Remission (brown), as well as an almost-white filly in 1981, he sired a sabino full sister in 1982. From Lots of Speed (brown), Khaleben sired the 1986 sabino colt, Colourful Gambler.
  Colourful Gambler, a B-grade showjumper, has 'red and bluish spots like ink thrown at him' and was registered in the Australian Stud Book as 'white'. Colourful Gambler has only ever sired two normal-coloured foals. Four are extensive or completely white, from Hanoverian mares, and there is a coloured 1997 filly from the Thoroughbred mare Like a Drop (by Live Arrow). This filly, Like a Gambler, is half chestnut and half white, but has been recorded in the stud book as white.
- Glenmaggie—1977 filly, colour not listed, by Khalif. Glenmaggie became the dam of two grey fillies from eight foals, both of which were by non-grey sires, proving that Glacial also carried the greying gene from her sire Grey Marwin.

The Bride 1991, white, born in Australia, originally with coloured ears and poll cap, by Star Shower from Saloeneo. Star Shower is known to have sired high white, and horses with white flecks/

speckles through the coat. In 1997, The Bride foaled a black/grey filly by a grey stallion, her first foal.

Our White Lady 1991, born in Australia, by Brazen Bay from Moncharm, both chestnuts. A white filly with a few chestnut flecks about her ears, poll and base of the tail.

CASE STUDY II: SABINO-WHITE FAMILY

Ron and Dorothy Childs run a well-known Pinto stud in South Australia. One of their most successful foundation lines has been the descendants of the sabino grade mare Rondoro Minnie Ha Ha. She has been a prolific producer of coloured foals. All the foals born sabino-white have shown some colour on the ears, top of head, along the spine and running into the tail. The colour was dark on some, and pale on the others. The colour is lost upon change of foal coat, except in the tail which

takes longer to grow out. Stallions used include the Arabian marginal chestnut sabino Nachoir, and the part Arabian tobiano Rondoro Capri (pictured on page 98), both registered Pintos. Curiously, from this family, sabino × sabino has never produced sabino, only sabino-white or normal solid.

CASE STUDY III: WHITE ARABIANS

The first registered all-white Arabian with pink skin and normal eyes was the colt Boomori Simply Stunning, bred by the Boomori Stud in Australia in 1989 of the two bays Chip Chase Kaiwanna and Crown Jewel. This pedigree is highly inbred to the stallions Raktha and Riffal, the latter line being known in Australia as one of the few that could occasionally produce brown or black Arabians. Indeed, this Boomori horse is also inbred to the mare Brown Anne, by Riffal, in the second and third generations.

Colourful Gambler, ASB Thoroughbred sabino

This colt appeared to be perfectly normal and was at first thought to be sabino-white. He later developed repigmentation spots on many areas of his body. Subsequent breeding from the horse produced five pure-bred Arabian white foals from five matings in his only crop (1993), only two of which were normal. The others exhibited neurological disorders and hypersensitivity and died within a few hours.

The production record of the colt does not fit any accepted genetic factor. If he were a rare mutation to dominant white, one would expect a non-white, normal coloured foal in the five matings. It is most likely he is a white mutation, although not of the normal dominant white (W^W) mechanism. This still does not explain why he produced 100 per cent white, some of which are defective when he himself is normal. It is probably due to a dominant gene

which is variable in expression. The two white daughters, Just a Dream and Meadow View Ivory Dream have shown dark repigmentation spots, especially about the face. Meadow View Ivory Dream also shows repigmentation under her tail. Just a Dream is from a bay mare. Her skin colour

---

Summary of matings of descendants of *Rondoro Minnie Ha Ha*

Sabino × solid*   15 matings
   result: 6 solids, 7 sabino, 2 sabino-white
Sabino × sabino*   14 matings
   result: 5 solid, nil sabino, 9 sabino-white
Sabino-white × solid   1 mating
   result: 1 sabino
Sabino-white × sabino   1 mating
   result: 1 sabino-white

Footnote to table

---

*Tobiano has been included with solid; tobino included with sabino.

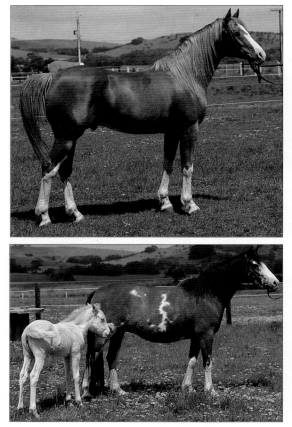

'The Rondoro horses': TOP: *Pure Arabian Nachoir, with belly patch on navel.* BOTTOM: *Foundation mare, Rondoro Minnie Ha Ha with sabino-white filly at foot by Nachoir*

TOP: *The four full sisters resulting from the mating with Nachoir.* BOTTOM: *Rondoro White Cloud, tobino daughter of Rondoro Minnie Ha Ha, with tobiano foal at foot, by Rondoro Capri*

Rondoro Chilali and sabino-white foal Rondoro Christel, by Rondoro Capri. The colour in the mane and ears has grown out

is darker, more orange in tone, and of a tougher quality than the skin of Meadow View Ivory Dream, who is from a chestnut mare. Meadow View Ivory Dream's skin colour is quite pink and rain scalds/sunburns readily, with subsequent peeling all over and other sensitivities. The two fillies are quite different in coat shade when seen together.

In 1996, Just a Dream foaled a white colt with chestnut patch on his poll and ears, which unfortunately has since died. Autopsy revealed severe ulceration of the gut. Meadow View Ivory Dream

died in 1997 from an allergic reaction to wormer. Camille Rogers, breeder of the two white fillies, says that an interesting feature of the three white horses is their particularly waxy coats. She likens it to an Australian white cockatoo, which 'if you touch, before long your hand is covered by a white powdery substance'.

ABOVE: *Just a Dream, all white Arabian (photo R. Flynn)*
LEFT: *Meadow View Ivory Dream, all white Arabian (photo R. Flynn)*

PART 6

SPOTTED PATTERNS

Family of true leopards

21

SPOTTED HORSES

Quick Guide: Spotting

- Spotting occurs in many forms in many breeds.
- All horses carrying the spotting gene will show 'characteristics' or mottling.
- Spotted-bred horses without characteristics have lost the spotting factor.
- The spotting factor is dominant and must be present before other spotting patterns can be exhibited.
- The patterns are dark spots, white spots, snowcap and varnish, each under the control of a separate dominant gene.
- Some of the patterns mimic one another, making identification difficult.
- The extent of visible spotting is dependant on modifying genes and the number of pattern genes.
- The greater the number of patterns in the parents, the higher percentage colour production.
- All spotting patterns may be safely bred to one another.
- The true few-spot leopard gives colour 100 per cent of the time.

There are many breeds of spotted horse throughout the world but none as well known as the Appaloosa. Indeed, the spotted pattern is now more often simply referred to as 'appaloosa'. The spotted coat may be one of the most primitive patterns in the horse. Researchers call this type of spotting the 'leopard complex' to distinguish it from the various white, pinto and roan coats that may have spots and patches. In Europe it is known as 'tiger spotting'. The true spotted horse is quite easy to distinguish with a little practice. All true spotted horses will have one or more of the distinctive features known as the 'characteristics'.

These are the minimum characteristics that must be present before identification as a spotted horse can be made. The narrow, vertically striped bands on the hooves are quite distinctive, unless white socks occur. For this reason the Appaloosa is generally shown with a natural, unblackened hoof. Solid, non-Appaloosa bred horses will occasionally show vertically striped hooves but these stripes will be relatively broad, originating from a white or ermine spotted coronary band. The hooves of

Characteristics of Appaloosa spotting pattern

- White sclera of the eye—present at birth;
- Mottled skin pigmentation on the face and/ or genitalia—present in only one-third of foals at birth and acquired later; and
- Striped hooves—present at birth.

chestnut, palomino and taffy horses can sometimes show less distinct narrow stripes resembling a spotted horse's hoof.

Clearly, some non-Appaloosa horses will have a white sclera, the visible white ring around the iris, but they will not have the associated striped hooves or mottled skin pigmentation. The mottled skin pigmentation is one of the best indicators in 'solid' spotted horses. Another occasional characteristic is the scanty mane and tail, or rat's tail, which is less common nowadays due to selective breeding.

The three characteristics, together known as *mottled*, are caused by gene Ap^{Ap} which is dominant and without which all the classic spotting patterns cannot be expressed. They are controlled by further modifiers which either determine the type of spotting present or determine the position, number and extent of the spotting.

These modifiers are known as quantitive or additive traits because the more modifiers present, the more extensive will be the colour. A horse with the Ap^{Ap} gene, but without modifiers, would merely show characteristics without colour, and a horse with many modifiers but without Ap^{Ap} would show neither colour nor characteristics. In addition, it is known that colts colour up more readily than fillies so Ap^{Ap} may be sex influenced. This could occur as follows:

Sex influence in the Appaloosa

Genotype	stallions	mares
$Ap^{Ap}Ap^{Ap}$	'false snowflake'	mottled
$Ap^{Ap}Ap^{+}$	mottled	minimal characteristics
$Ap^{+}Ap^{+}$	solid	solid

Modifiers control the position, spread and number of patterns by placing colour on the rump, much of the body, or (with more modifiers) extending colour to the whole body. There are no discrete differences, rather the markings occur over a continuum. Spot size is also controlled by modifiers.

Modifiers act somewhat like a committee, each having a small effect, but together there is a great deal of influence. Sometimes the spots tend to merge together, creating a patchy effect, but this may be

due to non-genetic factors such as 'developmental noise' (environmental effects in utero) and hormones.

The spotted coat is the most complex of all the equine patterns to understand and not a lot is known about its inheritance. An early model of Appaloosa inheritance was proposed by Miller around 1965, following a study of some thousands of horses, and others have proposed ideas based on studies in mice. Miller found that the most common spotting pattern in Appaloosas at that time was the 'roan' or varnish. Sponenberg (1990) provided information from several breeds in which he looked at data from the crossing of spotted horses with solids. The only difficulty in interpreting this data was that no distinction was made between white, varnish and spotted blankets, nor were the crosses made with solid horses of non-spotted backgrounds. However, a loose order of dominance was found.

LEFT: *Striped Appaloosa hoof (other hoof not striped due to presence of white sock)*
BELOW: *Mottling or false snowflake in a colt that was not a good colour producer*

Near leopard, with solid colour on mane, tail and legs

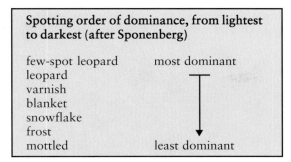

Spotting order of dominance, from lightest to darkest (after Sponenberg)	
few-spot leopard	most dominant
leopard	
varnish	
blanket	
snowflake	
frost	
mottled	least dominant

Sponenberg found that:

- Few-spot × few-spot produced all patterns except mottled, that is 100 per cent colour;
- Leopard × leopard produced all patterns;
- Varnish × varnish, and blanket × blanket, produced all patterns except few-spot, leopard and mottled;
- Frosted horses produced only the varnish;
- Snowflake horses produced leopard, blanket and snowflake foals; and
- All patterns, except few-spot, mated to solid, produced solid 50 per cent of the time.

I have endeavoured to provide workable suggestions on Appaloosa heredity for Appaloosa breeders, based on discussion with the breeders themselves. Basically, this model is multifactorial and proposes four patterns: snowcap (or blanket), dark spots, white spots and varnish.

SNOWCAP

Snowcap refers to the Sc^s allele which prevents pigment formation so that white appears. The horse is born with this pattern and changes very little, if at all. This gene is incompletely dominant but in homozygous form, $Sc^s Sc^s$, produces the few-spot.

A horse with Sc^s but no other forms of spotting genes would have a white patch with underlying pink skin over the hips, known as a snowcap or white blanket; the white can extend to the withers when it is known as 'snowcap to withers'. Snowcap white can even cover most of the body, in which case the horse would still have some colour on the head and legs, girth, flanks, and in the tail, as in the photograph.

The few-spot is true breeding. In spite of the fact that it is so white as to have very few spots and does not look like a classic Appaloosa, the few-spot is a breeder's greatest tool for colour production because it gives 100 per cent Appaloosa colour. Many horses are incorrectly described as few-spot when in fact they have large snowcaps with dark head, neck and tail. The true few-spot leopard will be white all over with, perhaps, dark flash markings on the legs. It is always born its adult colour.

It is not a very well known fact that one of the associated (pleiotropic) effects of the snowcap pattern in the few-spot leopard is the incidence of night blindness. The incidence of night blindness in ordinary horses is likely to be as high as one in

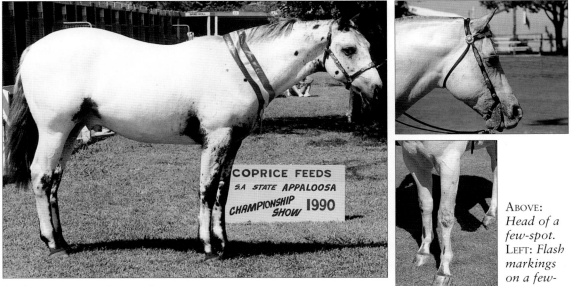

ABOVE: *Snowcap white or few-spot*

ABOVE: *Head of a few-spot.* LEFT: *Flash markings on a few-spot*

(a) white blanket

(b) white blanket

(c) snowcap over rump
or white blanket

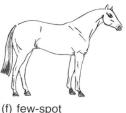

(d) snowcap to withers
or white blanket

(e) large snowcap

(f) few-spot

FIGURE 21.1 *Gradients of snowcap*

Spotted blanket, showing spots following the direction of the hair

sixteen, but in the few-spot leopard it is thought that 100 per cent are night blind to a greater or lesser degree. To what extent the condition occurs in snowcaps is not known.

DARK SPOTS

Dark spots refers to the Sd^s allele which causes dark spots sometimes as large as a fist. These are usually present at birth. Over the lifetime of the horse they may 'migrate', disappear or reappear. There is no visible difference between the homozygote and heterozygote.

Dark spots in the Appaloosa are not perfectly round; the larger they are the more they take on an oval shape. They frequently have 'roan' edges giving a halo effect, although this is often dependent on the length of the coat. It is interesting to note that the spots follow the direction of the hair, more oblique or horizontal over the quarters; and more nearly vertical in the flank, over the neck and forequarters. The texture of the hair varies with the white and dark spots, such that some say they can feel the spots.

Spots on the lower legs are known as *flash markings*. Dark spots can occur on their own, but are usually only evident in conjunction with other patterns such as snowcap, thus giving rise to the spotted blanket and leopard patterns.

A horse with Sd^s and no other spotting genes would have dark spots over the hips or even over the entire body, which may pass unnoticed in a dark-coloured horse. The spots would be the same colour as the base colour or darker. For example, a chestnut horse may have chestnut or liver spots but never sorrel spots. It is not known why this occurs although various explanations have been put forward.

The best way to study the leopard complex might be to look at spotted mules, because the donkey could be assumed to be a true solid. Appaloosa horses bred to donkeys would result in mules displaying all patterns except the few-spot.

SNOWFLAKE (WHITE SPOTS)

Snowflake refers to the Sn^s allele which causes small speckles (lace) and white spots about the size of a coin. The horse may not show the spots at birth, but they become increasingly evident with age and may shift position or 'migrate', or disappear and reappear. There is no visible difference between the homozygote and heterozygote. A horse with Sn^s, but no other forms of spotting, would be solid coloured with white spots which, when only on the hips, are known as lace blanket or frost; if covering most of the body, are known as snowflake. It is possible that snowflake and mottling are modifications of the same gene Ap^{Ap}, but here they are treated separately. It is uncertain whether an all-white snowflake could occur.

VARNISH

Varnish refers to the Sv^s allele, a non-spotting gene which causes a varnish or progressive 'silvering' effect, with colour remaining on bony prominences. Homozygous varnish is thought to be much lighter than heterozygous varnish, but still retains colour on the head.

Sometimes called 'marble-roan', varnish looks a bit like roan. Unlike roan it fades or silvers out with age, usually from two to six years. This is a slow process, but unlike grey there is usually no pigment loss from any spots present. Many varnish

Appaloosas are born solid-coloured, with just Appaloosa characteristics and varnish over the forehead. The silvering process can occur over the whole horse or just over the rump, where it is often mistaken for frost but would more correctly be called 'varnish blanket'.

(a) snowflake blanket (frost)

(b) snowflake

(c) extensive snowflake

FIGURE 21.2 *Gradients of snowflake*

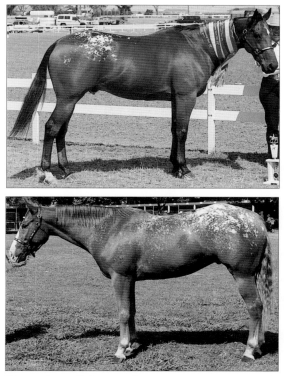

UPPER: *Snowflake over hips*
LOWER: *Snowflake over upper body*
RIGHT: *Extensive snowflake. Notice in full snowflake there is very little spotted colour on the head*

A typical varnish, say black varnish, would have blue/black areas remaining like smudges about the hips, stifle, forearm, lower neck and bony prominences of the face. The horse would be born black with perhaps black-spotted blanket and varnish over the forehead, and gradually turns through 'blue' to almost white.

Crop-out spotting

The spontaneous appearance of spotted horses (crop-outs) in breeds whose colour restrictions disallow such colours has been a problem for geneticists and breeders. Early foundation breeders of the Quarter Horse sometimes inadvertently bred from horses carrying the varnish gene, as many of these horses were described or registered as roan. Many of the crop-out Appaloosas, such as the famous Joker B, trace to the stallion Arab, which was a leopard, and many of Arab's descendants were also registered Quarter Horses, especially those minimally marked or thought to be roan.

It is important to realise that although the spotted colour may appear to skip generations when tracing pedigrees of registered horses, the spotting gene for mottle or varnish is always present in one or other of the parents (just as it is with the four pinto patterns in one of the parents of crop-out Paints).

Varnish Appaloosa Just Jake. Here the darker colour in the bony prominences of the head is interrupted by the large blaze

The Appaloosa colour patterns	
Pattern	Controlling gene
Appaloosa characteristics (mottled)	Ap^{Ap}
Snowcap (white blanket)	Sc^{s}
Dark spots	Sd^{s}
Snowflake (white spots)	Sn^{s}
Varnish	Sv^{s}

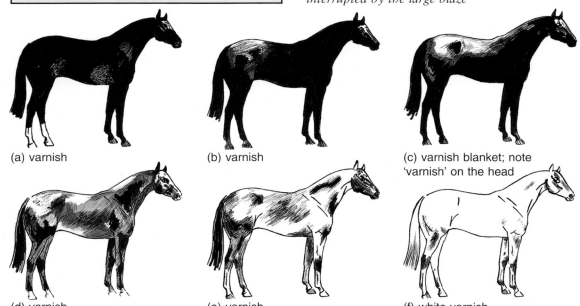

(a) varnish

(b) varnish

(c) varnish blanket; note 'varnish' on the head

(d) varnish

(e) varnish

(f) white varnish

FIGURE 21.3 *Gradients of varnish. A horse may stay in one stage, or fade out through several phases*

UNDERSTANDING APPALOOSA GENOTYPES

Using the chart below, it is possible to design matings which will result in colour from apparently solid horses, provided one parent is chosen from each column. It is possible, although less likely, for non-spotted bred horses to have the genotypes of column 2.

I knew a mottled horse in the early days of Quarter Horse breeding in this country, which was a pure-bred of imported parents (one parent mottled although spotted characteristics were not permitted within the breed, and presumably of column 1 genotype).

Spotted horses (Ap^{Ap}_) were unknown in Australia at that time. Although this Quarter Horse colt showed spotted characteristics, the significance of this was not revealed until he sired a snowflake colt from a station mare, then a minimal snowflake colt from a stud book Thoroughbred mare. The first snowflake son went on to sire several spotted foals including a blanket, although his percentage colour production was very low. This suggests some of the solid mares contributed to the variation of patterns in the progeny.

Examples of genotypes for solid horses of spotted background
$^+$ represents the normal allele for non-spotted

1 With characteristics	2 Without characteristics
$Ap^{Ap}\_Sc^+Sc^+$	$Ap^+Ap^+Sc^S\_$
$Ap^{Ap}\_Sd^+Sd^+$	$Ap^+Ap^+Sd^S\_$
$Ap^{Ap}\_Sn^+Sn^+$	$Ap^+Ap^+Sn^S\_$
$Ap^{Ap}\_Sv^+Sv^+$	$Ap^+Ap^+Sv^S\_$

COMBINATION PATTERNS

Of course, many Appaloosas display a combination of patterns—white patch, dark spots visible on the white patch, and white snowflakes visible on the base colour. Such horses are higher percentage colour producers.

When describing a spotted horse, the base colour should be mentioned first, then the type of spots and size of pattern such as:
- Black with black-spotted blanket;
- Chestnut snowflake with white blanket;

- Tri-colour near leopard (with bay and black spots);
- Red dun with frost and dark spots over body;
- Palomino true leopard; or
- Bay with lace blanket.

In cases such as the leopard, the base colour will be identified by the colour of the spots and the colour in the mane and tail, when not pure white. The mane will be white except where coloured hairs originate from spots on the top of the neck; black hairs in the case of bay, and red in the case of chestnut. A tri-colour leopard would be bay if it shows red and black spots. A chestnut leopard will have red spots.

UPPER: *Snowflake and spotted blanket*
LOWER: *Cremello with dark spots over body*

What is the difference between true leopard and false leopard?
Dark spots and the snowcap gene together gives spotted blanket, near leopard or true leopard, with or without dark background colour in the legs, head and tail. Spotted blanket bred to spotted blanket results in colour about 75 per cent of the time, including leopard.

ABOVE: *Spotted buckskin, showing loss of colour impact due to the dilution factor*
BELOW: *Airbrush blanket, snowcap, dark spots, and maybe varnish. Mighty Storm Song (imp.USA) (photo S. McAuliffe)*

Dark spots and the varnish gene can fade out to a pattern similar to leopard. These are false leopards which can be very difficult to distinguish from true leopard. True leopard is born leopard (including the face) and stays leopard. Background colour nearly always remains in the head, knees and hips of the false leopard. Colour at birth is the deciding factor. True leopard will always be a better breeding proposition than the false leopard.

RESPONSIBILITIES OF THE APPALOOSA BREEDER

The aim of the Appaloosa breeder is to produce a unique colour with much contrast to preserve the identity of the breed. For this reason outcrossing with grey or roan is prohibited in Australia, and base colours are preferred over the dilute colours. Two dilute Appaloosas should never be bred together as there is always the possibility of producing a cremello or a spotted cremello, which is difficult to sell, although it may be useful in producing palomino Appaloosas. Horses of spotted breeding are generally prohibited for use in other breeds' upgrading programs due to possible recurrence of spotted patterns.

Also to be considered as unsatisfactory is the horse with excessive white or minimal sabino characteristics. White socks can be attractive, but high white, although not disallowed, can ultimately lead to the production of a sabino/spotted combination. Horses showing pinto markings are not permitted in the Appaloosa breed. It is recommended that any horse showing high white be bred to a total solid, or at least to a horse of limited white markings, so that classic sabino does not become an established pattern. Breeds of spotted horse throughout the world include the Appaloosa, Australian Palouse Pony, Austrian Pinzgauer or Noriker, British Spotted Horse, Colorado Ranger, Danish Knabstrup, the Harlequin Horse (a US breed of spotted Warmblood), the Libyan Leopard, and the Pony of the Americas. Very rarely, spotting occurred in the Andalusian, Lusitano, Shetland and Welsh Pony, but because of negative selection, may have disappeared altogether from these breeds.

PART 7

MODIFYING
PATTERNS

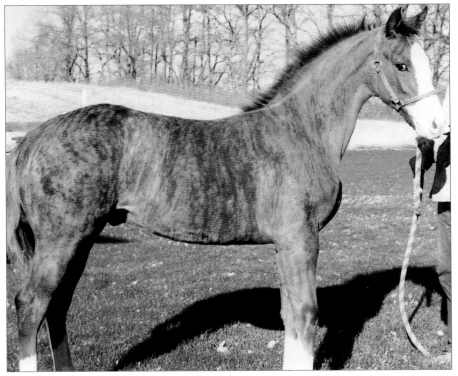

Brindle Quarter Horse colt Dunbar's Gold at five months of age (photo © D. Dunbar). This American Quarter Horse colt appears to be chestnut or red dun with dark red stripes which are also growing through the mane

22

OTHER COLOURS AND MODIFICATIONS

BRINDLE

Brindle is an extremely rare pattern of striping in horses. No formal published study has been done. The brindle colouration is quite different from a dun with extensive zebra striping and should not be confused with it. It is more like the brindle colour seen in dogs, cats and Jersey cattle, and nothing like the markings of a zebra.

Brindle is a pattern of vertical, roughly parallel stripes found all over the body, also on both sides of the neck and extending down the legs almost to the knee and hock joint. The heaviest concentrations are on the forequarters, neck and hindquarters, where the stripes are crowded together. Each stripe varies in width and character. Some are more squiggly, others more blotchy and merging in to one another. A comprehensive treatment of the brindle horse can be found at website http://members.aol.com/ brindlehos under 'Brindle horses—a rare equine coat color' written by Sharon Batteate, who has been researching the pattern since 1990. I quote extracts with her permission.

Brindle mare Brenda Batty Atty (owner/photo J. Sharon Batteate)

Striping and camouflage in horses

Camouflage, or protective colouration, in horses and other animals has taken many forms. In general, animals from forest or woodland environments tend to be darker, often with sections of the coat forming into spotted or striped patterns which mimic the effect of light filtering through trees. Animals from desert environments tend towards the yellowish, tan, or red hues, often with an agouti pattern in which each individual hair is striped or banded (rather than entire sections of the coat being striped), so that the animal now ap-

pears a non-striped, single colour (monochrome), which blends better with sandy soils. Generally, there seems to be a tendency toward the non-striped agouti/monochrome colouration.

Animals also migrate into different environments from which root stock originally evolved. In these cases, the adults may eventually evolve and develop protective colouration to match their surroundings, but the young are often still born with the original primitive patterns from which they evolved. An example of this is the tapir, a living relative of the horse.

Adult tapirs appear non-striped, but the young are born with light stripes on the body. Young lions are born with spotted and striped patterns, but become single/monochrome coloured when they mature. Similarly, sometimes horse foals are born with primitive patterns and striping, which they lose as they mature.

Striping is believed to be the most ancient form of camouflage, and is believed to precede both spotted and monochrome type patterns. A striped appearance can be caused in several ways. One is by the clumping of darker pigmented areas into streaks, as seen in the stripes of tabby cats and tigers, and also in the dorsal stripes and barring on the legs of donkeys and dun factor horses. A striped appearance can also be achieved by the introduction of lighter or white bands of hair, as seen in zebras, nyala, okapi, and other types of antelopes, and in some roan horses.

Spotting patterns are produced from the disintegration or breaking up of stripes. Often spots are clearly arranged in rows, so you can still see the pattern of the original stripe. Civet cats are good examples of this, and often have stripes on the head, but spots on the body. In some leopard Appaloosa horses, the spots also seem to form broken-up stripes. The quagga, an extinct form of zebra, was characterised by having stripes primarily only on the head and neck. On the body, the stripes were broken down into a wavy or mottled pattern, and then finally became a reddish brown monchrome pattern.

Monochrome and agouti-like patterns result from the further breakdown of spots and stripes, so the body of the animal now appears to be mostly a single uniform colour, although the face and back may still show some evidence of mottling or striping. Abyssinian cats are good examples of this process, as well as the above mentioned quagga. Most of our horses today also exhibit monochrome type patterns, although on dun factor horses, some of the primitive striping still remains on the legs and down the back. The rest of the body, however, has gone the way of the quagga, with any primitive striping having disintegrated into a monochrome pattern.

Another ancient camouflage technique is countershading. The animal is coloured darker along the topline, and paler below, in order to counteract shadows caused by natural overhead light (which lights the top but causes shadows on the underside making the animal look three dimensional). Even on zebras, the stripes are widest on the back, and smaller as they move toward the underside, so they exhibit countershading as well as disruptive striping for camouflage. In horses, the darker topline seen on mahogany bays and in the 'seal brown' pattern, and the coloured back and sides, but almost white belly of the 'blonde sorrel' pattern, are examples of countershading.

Zebra

There is not much genetic information available on striping for horses, but in mice, there are at least six different loci which produce striping patterns (usually called mottling in mice). The International Striped Horse Association collects information and registers horses with striped patterns, and studies various striping patterns in horses. It can be reached at PO Box 209, Silver Cliff, CO 81249 USA.

Brindle horses

The first record of the brindle pattern in horses seems to be by J.A. Lusis, in the publication Genetica vol. 23, 1942. In the article on 'Striping Patterns in Domestic Horses', he details a Russian cab horse from around the 1800s, that was preserved and put in the Zoological Museum of the Academy of Sciences of the USSR, in Leningrad. I believe the horse is now in the Natural History Museum in St. Petersburg, Russia. Brindle has occurred in such diverse breeds as Arabians, Thoroughbreds, mustangs, Quarter Horses, Bavarian Warmbloods, Russian horses, Spanish horses, and supposedly in the Netherlands. In the Criollo horses of Argentina, 'gateado' (dun color), sometimes has a variation known as 'gateado barcino' or brindle dun.

Many people confuse dun factor markings (stripe down the back, barring on the legs) with brindle. Indeed, there have been many examples of horses that were probably carrying both genes. However, the Russian cab horse, and the brindle mare in the photo [on page 110] do not have any dun factor markings whatsoever. Brindle horses also have texturing in their coat, similar to that seen in some Appaloosa horses. The pattern seems to be inheritable, especially in terms of coat texturing, but the extent of striping is highly variable.

In the past when a brindled foal was born, they were considered a random mutation, were often considered undesirable (since they were not a normal color within many breed or registry guidelines), and were often gelded or sold without papers. It was reported that the pattern was not reproducable.

However, given the lack of knowledge about the pattern and the seeming prejudice against it, that is not surprising. While some brindles may occasionally occur due to a random mutation, I feel the brindle pattern could also have been carried from ancient times, perhaps in a manner similar to striping in cats.

All cats carry some form of striping, but will not show it unless they also have the agouti gene. If you look closely at a black cat (which doesn't have the agouti gene), you can still see the striping as a form of 'ghost' markings in the coat. However, most people don't notice the ghost markings, and only see a black cat.

I feel something similar may be happening with the brindle pattern, and that it takes the right combination of genes to produce a visible pattern. Brindle carriers could go unnoticed, either because the markings are assumed to be part of the dun factor pattern, or in other cases, because brindle seems to cause a coat texturing, but without obvious striping, and can thus be overlooked.

These horses when bred, would occasionally pick up the right combination of genes needed to produce visibly brindled offspring, which would then seem to have cropped out from unmarked parents.

However, the above is speculation on my part, only intended to furnish some kind of starting point, as we really don't know very much. That is why we are looking for horses for a study. When Dunbar's Gold [page 109] is old enough to start breeding (1998), it will be especially important to track his offspring. The AQHA rule change to allow shipping of cooled semen will now make it very easy to breed to him.

Brindle horses are usually registered with the Buckskin societies as brindle dun. While accepting that some brindles have occurred in non-dun breeds in the past (probably due to random mutation), recent cases appear to have dun parentage suggesting brindle could be an aberration of dun.

Champagne black Australian Quarter Horse

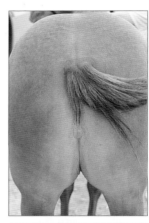

LEFT: *Rear view of champagne black shows skin colour.* ABOVE: *Head of champagne black shows hazel eye and freckled skin*

Pink-skinned golden palomino American Saddlebred, Barrister Farm's Wild Thing, as a foal had blue eyes and red-tinged mane. See mature horse on page 122

CHOCOLATE—THE B^b ALLELE

Some geneticists cite the very rare chocolate colour with light brown skin and amber eyes as evidence of the existence of B^b in horses.

Chocolate brown pigmentation is normally controlled by the B^b allele in other species. Dark chocolate is a colour seen in donkeys, but there is little evidence to suggest the colour occurs in horses. Chances are that the few reported horses of this shade are in reality liver chestnut or dark champagne black (see below).

CHAMPAGNE—THE CH^C ALLELE

The inheritance of this rare colour group is the result of a dominant dilution gene which Sponenberg (1996) has named the *Champagne* locus. The champagne gold, champagne black and champagne buckskin are the only colours in the horse where pink skin produces anything other than white hairs. All horses with pink skins discussed so far have been the result of the double dilution $C^{Cr}C^{Cr}$ and are cremello or perlino. Intercrossing of champagnes is thought not to produce a cremello/perlino equivalent, and should produce homozygous champagnes; however due to the rarity of the colour, homozygotes have yet to be reported.

Champagne dilutes black to reddish or silvery chocolate, and red to gold. Champagnes have a marked tendency to iridescence and reverse dapples. The eyes, at birth, are nearly always white or pale blue, but darken with greenish flecks until they turn amber around three months of age.

As all the champagne colours are quite rare, existing only in the herds of specialised breeders, little is known as to origins, or the results in combination with other colours. The colour is most commonly recognised in American Saddlebreds and Tennessee Walkers, and has been documented in other breeds of Spanish origin.

Champagne gold (wheaten-skinned palomino)
This impressive colour looks identical to true palomino, but is accompanied by a pink, brownish-pink or pumpkin coloured skin. It has marked iridescence and is often accompanied by a gold or reddish mane and tail rather than the true white. There is a freckle-skinned variety, where the skin is dotted with pink and dark speckles (misnamed 'mottled' by Palomino registries) and a completely pink-skinned variety.

Wheaten-skinned palominos regularly produce a chestnut described as 'cherry' when bred to one another. Some matings produce both pink-skinned and dark-skinned palomino progeny.

'Cremellos' resulting from dark and pink-skinned palomino crosses tend to be a rich cream rather than the pale off-white of normal cremellos. They have a mottled skin and greenish flecks through their eyes. Sponenberg has called these ivory champagnes. They are not true cremellos at all; rather they are mimics, resulting from a composite of both champagne and a single cremello dilute.

Some palomino breeders feel that they get a higher percentage of gold colour production from using pink-skinned palominos than from using the normal dark-skinned palomino, with less incidence of faulty colour such as smuts. This would be true given that the *Champagne* locus does not produce cremellos. It is also highly likely that champagne dilutes out or inhibits smuts.

The pink-skinned cream is found in the endangered American Cream Draft Horse, and the pink-skinned golden is found in the American Saddlebred and Tennessee Walking Horse breeds. The Palomino Horse Breeders Association of America registers only pink-skinned palominos if they are American Saddlebreds. The wheaten-skinned palomino is not found in Australian horse breeds.

Champagne buckskin (wheaten-skinned buckskin)
The champagne combination with bay and brown base colours gives the champagne buckskin, which Sponenberg calls 'amber champagne'.

Champagne black
The horse shown here is the rare champagne black, more routinely called simply 'champagne'. It has been referred to formerly as 'lilac dun', a term used by Sponenberg (1983). The horse is not really a dun at all because the *Dunning* gene D^D is not present and leg barrings are not seen. The colour is pale smoky brown or shimmering lilac/silver rather like a Weimeraner dog, with pinkish brown skin and darker smoky chocolate points. The eyes are amber. The foals are born with deep blue eyes.

Case study: Champagne family
A wonderful line of Tennessee Walking Horses started with the 1969 champagne mare Champagne Lady

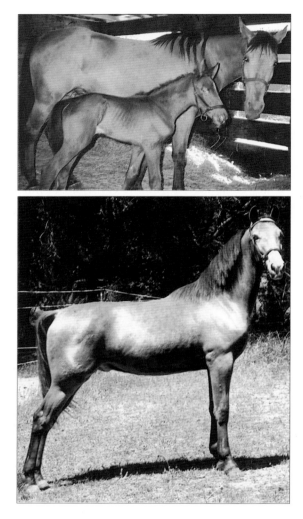

ABOVE LEFT: *Champagne Touché and foal Champagne Diane by Champagne Look*
LEFT: *Shades of Champagne, champagne colt by Champagne Look*
ABOVE: *Champagne Look*

- Pride's Champagne by Pride of Midnight H.F.—black colt
- Champagne Copy by Carbon Copy—champagne filly
- Champagne Night by Pride's Stormy Night—champagne colt
- 1988 black filly
- Champagne Look by Royal Senator—champagne colt

Diane (Johnny Midnight × Mac's Golden Girl H). Champagne Lady Diane is remembered not only for her unique colour but as a top show mare which won classes at 23 major shows in Tennessee for her owner Diane Green of Tullahoma. Her sire was black and her dam, although registered as yellow with flax mane and tail, has been described as a 'funny perlino-type colour' (which could mean she was ivory champagne).

Hair samples from Champagne Lady Diane were submitted by Diane Green to both the University of Tennessee at Knoxville and later to Auburn University at Auburn, Alabama. Both agreed Champagne Lady Diane's colour was unique. Champagne Lady Diane produced seven foals:

- Eb's Champagne Velvet—black filly
- Unnamed black colt which died through accident.

Pride's Champagne was described by the Greens as 'the greatest horse they'd ever raised', jet black, 16.2hh and could do 'a perfect four-beat running walk'. He was bought and used at stud by the Kinkades of Elk Grove, California, for several years before they sold him to buy Champagne Look. They later bred the black Pride's Champagne daughter Champagne Chance to Champagne Night to produce the champagne filly Champagne Touché.

Champagne Look is probably the best known champagne horse in the world, and Bea Kinkade is to be congratulated for her efforts to preserve this colour in the Tennessee Walking Horse breed, at a time when there were only three known in the world, all descendants of Champagne Lady Diane. The story of how she did this is recorded in the *Voice of the Tennessee Walking Horse* magazine, Souvenir Celebration Edition, August 1992.

It was Bea Kinkade who coined the term 'champagne' and was instrumental in having it recognised as a colour in its own right by the TWHBEA.

Bea Kinkade says: 'The champagne's coat is very short and fine in texture, with clear glass-like hairs, giving them an iridescent, metallic sheen. These horses never photograph their true color, often turning out greenish! Champagne Look even in the

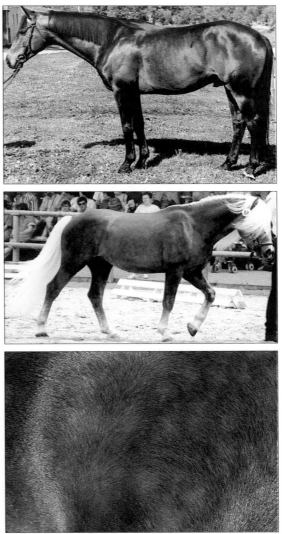

The Sooty gene is described on page 117.
TOP: *Golden brown Australian Stock Horse mare and brown foal, both with sooty gene, and foal with muzzle ring typical of pangaré*
BOTTOM: *Close-up of same foal, Chalani Gemini*

TOP: *Bay Australian Stock Horse stallion Fintona Artist with sooty gene and smuts.*
CENTRE: *Sooty chestnut Haflinger Waldstadt (photo J. Hele).* BOTTOM: *Dappled flank of chestnut with sooty gene producing 'false liver'*

dead of winter is always slick and shiny. And he is not kept blanketed or even in a stall.'

Champagne Look and his sons have produced champagnes out of all coloured mares, never getting a cremello, palomino, or any offspring with a light mane and tail. (He is homozygous black.) To the end of 1997 he had sired 33 champagnes and 18 blacks (one of these a black and white), with only two foals ever non-black or non-champagne. Both were bay. This is an unusual ratio, almost 2:1 champagne to not champagne, and is also unusual in the number of resulting blacks, since well over half the matings were to bay, chestnut or palomino mares which can be presumed to carry A locus genes. Ordinarily this would give many more than two bay foals. Dominant black E^D may need to be considered here.

The first mating of champagne to champagne resulted in the champagne filly Champagne Diane, which carries a triple cross of the mare Champagne Lady Diane. Each of Champagne Lady Diane's sons is represented in Champagne Diane's pedigree.

DOMINANT BLACK

The idea of a dominant black allele E^D has been suggested to explain certain anomalies in the colour breeding of some American Clydesdales, Tennessee Walkers and American Shetlands where, occasionally and extremely rarely, black bred to black has produced bay.

There is no evidence to support the existence of E^D in Australia and indeed most geneticists discount the existence of E^D completely. If E^D, or dominant black exists, we would get a jet black horse regardless of alleles of the A series.

Test breeding suspected E^D Tennessee Walkers with blacks of other pure breeds such as the Friesian (should get some bay foals), or bays as in the Cleveland Bay (should get some black foals) would confirm or refute this theory.

LETHAL DILUTE (LAVENDER FOAL)

This is a rare dilute coat pattern somewhat like buckskin, as described by Bowling (1996), and seen in Arabian foals. It is associated with difficult birth and is always lethal. The foal is unable to stand and nurse, and neurological disorders, including rapid eye movement and joint rigidity, occur. The defect is thought to be a simple recessive.

PANGARÉ

Sponenberg (1983) proposed a dominant allele for a horse with mealy muzzle. The strict meaning of pangaré (pronounced pang-ar-ie) is a dark red horse with light muzzle ring and underbelly. It is known in England as 'roebuck belly' or, less commonly, 'donkey nose'.

It should not be mistaken for the minor lightness in the soft parts which distinguishes a brown (A^t) from black (A^a). Pangaré is a diffuse light 'cast' which can come almost one-third of the way up the underbelly, insides of the legs, forearms and buttocks (hams) and nose/muzzle ring. If pangaré occurs around the eyes, as in Exmoor ponies, these are termed 'hooded' eyes.

Pangaré also lightens out the lower legs, especially in chestnuts. It may even cause a lighter mane and tail, so that in combination with F^fF^f, the mane and tail are white. Pangaré may be responsible for the extreme lightness of the blonde sorrel, which is always allied with pangaré.

In bays, the dark points are restricted sometimes to the fetlocks, and a mealy muzzle and underbelly are apparent. Pangaré brown is the golden brown, basically black with yellow underside, which is sometimes confused with sooty buckskin.

Crossbreeding the native dun with normal colours tends to suggest that in Fjords, at least, the muzzle ring is recessive. In this breed, pangaré has no effect on a black base colour, because *gra* never has a muzzle ring.

Some geneticists hold that pangaré alters a genetically black horse ($A^aA^aE^+\_$) to the seal-brown but this is unlikely to be the case in view of observations on the Fjord breed. Also, if pangaré created the seal-brown then bay × bay could not give brown, unless one of the bays had a muzzle ring, but this is not the case.

The mealy muzzle ring is virtually non-existent in Australian Arabians, and brown horses are uncommon. Data from Volume 1 of the *Australian Arabian Stud Book*, published in 1960, reveals that from 394 animals there was only one black, the colt Amaluka, bred from imported parents who are not described, and 12 browns.

All but two of these browns were sired by, or were descendants of, the well-known dark bay Riffal. Disregarding the few matings to grey or chestnut mares, all Arabian matings recorded in Volume 1 which produced brown were bay bred to bay. This supports the theory that brown is recessive to bay and is probably not caused by pangaré. In the Australian Pony breed, I have observed parents without muzzle ring produce progeny with muzzle ring, refuting the view that pangaré is dominant.

There is only one breed in the world where the light muzzle ring has been selectively bred in both bay and brown and this is the Exmoor, a very old breed in England.

Most have the mealy (yellow) muzzle but some rings are red (coppernose). Outcrossing the Exmoor should reveal information about pangaré in the crossbred progeny.

SEASONAL DAPPLING AND THE SOOTY GENE

Dapples are large, dark, interconnected, circular markings which occur primarily on the lower half of the body in some greys and the top half of the body in some taffies. Rarely, dapples are found over the entire body.

They can be as large as a fist or as small as a coin. On the whole, grey and taffy are the only two colours in which dappling is seen all year round. Dappling, when present in these colours, is an associated (pleiotropic) effect of G^G and Z^Z. We must distinguish between the more or less permanent dapples of the grey and taffy, and the seasonal nature of dapples in other colours, particularly in bays, browns, chestnuts and palominos.

Seasonal dapples are the result of the sooty factor, which also gives a darker overcast to the entire body. These dapples usually appear at first change of summer coat and fade away after some months. They are a response to good health, seasonal conditions and feeding regime. However, there is a certain genetic predisposition towards this as some horses never show dappling even in the best of health.

The inheritance of seasonal dappling has not been studied and it would be a difficult task given the sensitivity of dappling to environmental influences. It is likely that the sooty gene Sty^S is responsible for dappling in ordinary colours and has variable penetrance. Under this hypothesis, Sty^S would darken a bay horse to dappled bay or bay with a lot of black through the coat, often including a cast or smudge down the bridge of the nose. A brown horse would be dappled brown or almost black. Palomino and buckskin would be sooty with dapples.

The Sty^S gene affects the body more than the legs. It also creates a mask down the bridge of the nose. Chestnuts darkened by sooty hairs could be mistaken for liver, but the dappling on light pasterns would indicate the presence of Sty^S.

Normally light pasterns in chestnut are a result of pangaré ($P^p\_$) or the flaxen F^fF^f genotype, but $Sty^S\_$ chestnuts will have a normal mane and tail and no muzzle ring. Liver chestnut plus $Sty^S\_$ would give the black chestnut with liver pasterns. The clear colours would be recessive Sty^+Sty^+. Clear colours bred to clear colours always give clear colours. If sooty and flaxen occurred in the same horse, we would see the chestnut with 'grey' mane and tail, some sooty hairs through the coat, and sootiness superimposed on lighter lower legs.

MARBLE MARKINGS

Marble markings start as a cluster of white hairs on various locations along the spine between the withers and root of the tail. The white hairs spread into wiggly and disconnected lines which may appear to join up as the pattern progresses. The widest part of the pattern is usually between the hips or along the withers.

Slowly, as the number of white hairs increases, the lines appear to meet, forming irregular circles like veins in marble. The older the horse, the more widespread the markings become. In some parts of Australia this marking is popularly known as 'cat-backed' after the markings of the marsupial cat.

Because marble markings usually develop in the adult horse, many owners consider them to have appeared as the result of some environmental influence. I have asked owners about their horses and almost invariably the owner has some reason why the speckles have appeared—the saddle has rubbed, the rug fitted too tightly, the horse was sprayed inadvertently by a chemical spray, the horse is allergic to pine pollen and it shelters under pine trees . . . so the list goes on.

However, where the breeding is known, an inherited pattern may be observed. The photograph of Australia's famous Standardbred sire Aachen was taken about six months before he died and clearly shows the extent to which the marbling pattern may spread as the animal reaches old age.

The marking is unusual in that it rarely, if ever, is present in immature horses. Some do not show evidence of development until well into adulthood, say seven to eight years of age. Aachen is an

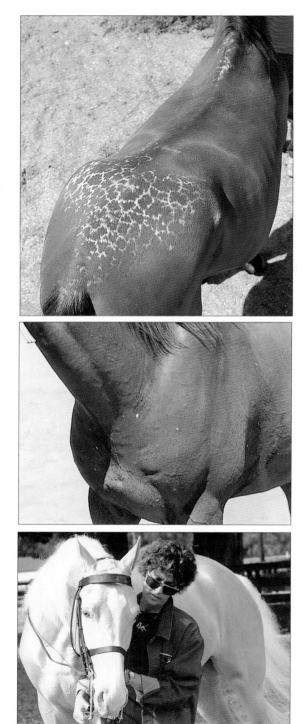

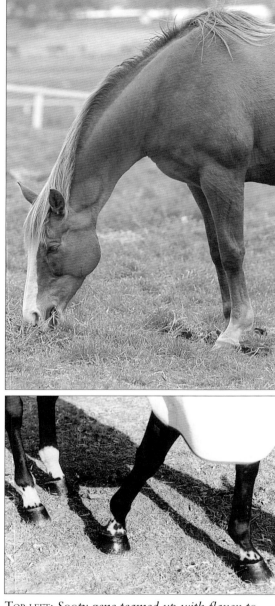

TOP LEFT: *Sooty gene teamed up with flaxen to give a 'grey' mane. This Thoroughbred will darken in spring to false liver with 'grey' mane*
BOTTOM LEFT: *Ermine spots on the socks of a Thoroughbred*
TOP RIGHT: *Marble markings on the Standard-bred Aachen*
CENTRE RIGHT: *Acquired spots*
BOTTOM RIGHT: *Amber eye of pink-skinned palomino Saddlebred*

White third eyelid in Warmblood

TOP: *Glass eye of cremello Australian Stock Horse*
CENTRE: *Wall eye appearing white in Fjord*
BOTTOM: *Wall eye appearing blue in Fjord*
RIGHT: *Eye of splashed white Miniature Horse 4 Go Fullers Equalizer (imp.USA) (photo M. Bennett)*

excellent example since he has sired so many foals. During his early racing days he showed no evidence of the marking. Yet at the twilight of his career a few speckled white hairs were visible near the withers and point of the rump. Nothing to take any notice of, since they were probably the result of wearing harness!

After Aachen was retired, and of course he no longer wore harness, the markings progressed. Year by year they increased, until at 29 years of age they had spread to the degree shown in the photo (see page 118). Marbling is so unusual, that one trotting fan said to me, if he ever saw the marking on a horse at the track he could safely conclude that it was by Aachen, or was a descendant of his.

Many of Aachen's sons and daughters exhibit marble markings to a lesser or greater degree. It appears to be inherited directly, rather than skipping generations. Other reports of marbling in ponies and Australian Stock Horses are confusing, often because the progeny are reported as having marbling before one of the parents itself shows the feature. This suggests simple dominance with variable penetrance: M^M for marbling, M^+ for non-marbling.

SPOTS

Acquired spots

Thumbnail sized white spots, which usually develop in young adult horses, are thought to be an inherited depigmentation, although there is no understanding of the mode of transmission. These spots tend to remain the same size although they may increase in number over the lifetime of the horse. Any colour may be affected. Sometimes acquired spots can be due to non-inherited causes, such as hair follicle damage from a virus or external parasites.

Ermine spots

Spots may be seen on the white socks of any breed of horse. They are highly prized because they usually appear on the coronary band and change what should have been a white hoof into a dark one, with its associated greater durability.

The spots are called ermine spots, ermine marks or 'distal leg spots'. They may be so pronounced as to make the sock appear 'dirty' or freckled. The inheritance has not been studied but it is probably dominant. They are frequently seen as a characteristic of tobianos, in Thoroughbreds, and are well known in the Freckles line of Quarter Horses.

Mismarks

A small or large patch of a non-inherited nature is referred to as a mismark. It may be white, or simply a lighter colour than the base colour. Rarely does the horse have more than one patch, and is otherwise normally marked. The horse is born with the patch, probably due to some developmental aberration. The mismark is not seen in the progeny. A mismark should be noted on registration papers for identification purposes.

Smuts

These are dark spots which can appear on horses of any colour but are particularly obvious on palominos and chestnuts. They can range from coin-sized to large patches taking in much of the shoulder, hip or chest.

They can often be seen on the knees and hocks first, before change in coat reveals more. Most spotting in horses is actually smuts, but few horses will have enough smuts to be considered 'spotted'. The inheritance is probably recessive.

The presence of smuts, also known as 'Bend Or spots' after the Thoroughbred of the same name, is closely allied to the type of feeding program the horse is on, so tends to be seasonal in appearance. Smuts are very common on the Welsh Pony.

EYE COLOUR

There is a great range of variation in the eye colour of horses. An occasional horse will have two differently coloured eyes. The normal eye is dark brown with brown sclera, iris and pupil (see the diagram on page 7).

In some lights the reflective qualities of the retina allow the pupil to look bluish, but this is normal. At night, the eyes of most horses reflect light as a yellow/green colour. Interestingly, the eye of the endangered Akhal-Teke is reported as reflecting light as a pink colour.

Sometimes the third eyelid will be pink, or off-white, distorting the normal appearance, or the sclera will be white.

This gives rise to the unfounded suspicion that such horses are of unreliable temperament. There is confusion here with a horse which is tense or afraid, which will roll its eyes and thus 'show the whites of its eyes'.

Appaloosa eye

This is actually a normal eye, but the ring around the pupil, known as the sclera, is white. Although this is an Appaloosa characteristic, it is by no means restricted to Appaloosas, and in particular, can be found on chestnuts with white on the face.

Frequently, the pigment loss associated with the white also occurs around the eyelids or, more extremely, on the face, resulting in the need for sun protection.

One of the most effective means of protection is blinkers, which can easily be sewn on to a leather halter by a saddler.

Hazel and amber eyes

These are lighter versions of the normal brown eye, found more commonly in chestnuts, palominos and buckskins. The iris is light brown and the pupil is dark as normal. The foal eye is often blue and darkens to amber later.

Yellow eye

The dilute eye when not amber or hazel is yellow or honey-coloured. Geurts (1977) describes the yellow eye as a distinguishing feature of the dilute black, but I have not seen this in Australia.

Glass eye

The eye of the pseudo-albino has an off-white/pale blue iris, with blue pupil, known as a glass eye. The sensitivity and eyesight of horses with glass eyes varies greatly.

Green, grey, and violet eyes

A green, grey or violet iris with normal brown pupil is rarely seen, but has been reported by breeders of Welsh Ponies and pinto horses.

Blue eye

This is a true deep dark blue all over—pupil and iris—and is a rare eye colour in horses. It may be so dark as to appear black with no pupil. In certain light the whole eye can appear almost like a black-red. I have only seen this eye colour in all-white horses.

Multi-coloured eye

This refers to horses whose eyes are flecked or speckled with two or more colours.

Wall eye

The wall eye has an off-white or light blue iris with normal dark brown pupil. Close examination of the eye reveals that dark blue appears to 'bleed' raggedly from the centre of the iris, spreading outward from the edge of the pupil into the iris. Elsewhere the iris is white.

The overall effect is of pale blue. The iris may also have small light blue patches 'floating' in it, rather like a horse that has suffered an eye injury. Wall eyes are very individual and it is probable that no two wall eyes are alike. Wall eye is occasionally associated with blindness due to iris hypoplasia.

The wall eye is most commonly seen in broken-coloured horses. Where it is seen in the occasional solid-coloured horse it appears to be recessive. One or both eyes may be affected.

Wall eye may be an indicator for some incomplete sabino, overo and tobiano horses. The splashed white always has two blue eyes and breeders believe the wall eye of the splashed white to be different from the wall eye of other horses, more of a grey-blue.

Wall eyes are often referred to as blue eyes, but they are also known as china eye, marble, chalk, or watch eye. Wall eyes have been reported in certain pure-bred strains of Arabian, such as those descending from Bazrah, or tracing further back to the mare Jerboa.

It need not be associated with excessive white, and may occur in horses with minimal white. Wall eye is possible in a total solid, but I have only seen it in ponies of tobiano ancestry.

The wall eye is quite different from an eye blinded through injury which has 'blued'. Wall eyes do not normally present a problem to the horse—rather they are simply an unsightliness.

A wall eye is unrelated to the cremello dilution and does not indicate the presence or otherwise of a pseudo-albino ancestor, nor the likelihood of the horse producing a pseudo-albino.

PART 8

MORE ABOUT

COLOUR

Wild Thing can be seen as a foal on page 112 in the previous chapter; here she is a mature performance horse, eyes changed to amber and mane to white (photo J. Schatzberg)

23

COLOUR CHANGES

Australian Stock Horse Chalani Caper as a foal (left) and a two-year old, (above) showing changes in the size of the star, mousy foal coat and mature colour

Ticking due to age

How often have you looked at your horse, wondering what colour it is exactly, only to find that it apparently changes colour with its new summer coat? Winter coats can even fool experts. That is why it is essential for your horse's colour to be identified when the horse is in good coat condition.

FACTORS AFFECTING COAT COLOUR

Age

A horse owner may be quite surprised to find that the long-awaited foal is not the colour it was expected to be. It may have strange, light grey eyes,

almost-pink skin and a pale coat. Particularly in foals born chestnut, the skin and eyes may take as long as a month to gain full pigment.

Foal coats tend to be 'mousy', a lighter version of the adult coat. This is nature's camouflage mechanism. A bay can be born so pale and with so little black on the legs that the owner thinks he has a chestnut. Sometimes, through the light cast, 'ghost' markings, shoulder stripes and leg barring can be seen, which usually disappear upon change of foal coat.

The foal coat will begin to change at about two months unless the foal was born out of season. First signs will appear around the eyes where the foal coat falls out, to be replaced by the new coat which will be the foal's adult colour. As the coat falls out over the neck and body, the foal becomes quite itchy (an ideal time for rubbing and handling), and the remaining coat becomes dull and yellowed. It may take some time before the dead hair falls out completely, giving a mottled and patchy appearance.

A mature horse's coat will usually be darker or richer than that of a yearling. The exception is grey, which will lighten with age. Dapples, too, may appear in the adult when they were not apparent in the young horse.

White markings in a foal can seem quite pronounced at birth. Frequently a marking will reduce over time, so that by two years old it loses its impact. In foals of Appaloosa parentage, a plain youngster may still colour up and the spots may even migrate over time. Horses' coats in old age tend to become dull in tone; many horses will show ageing by acquiring white hairs over the body, especially on the flanks and on the forehead. Ageing white, as distinct from true ticking, generally appears from about age 15 years onwards, but may not start till as late as 25 years.

Breed

Ponies and coldbloods tend to have paler coats than the same colour in hotblooded breeds. This is due to the length and thickness of the hair, which makes the coat slightly dull and more difficult to prepare. Some breeds have a dense undercoat which can be darker or lighter than the top coat; this coat can show through the top coat, giving the superficial appearance of a change in colour.

Climate

Horses which live in the greatest extremes of temperature between winter and summer will display the greatest changes in coat colour. Very few coats remain unaffected by the cold. Not only does the coat become longer, harsher and more upright, it can become distinctly paler or darker, especially in countries which experience snow. The undercoat may also be lighter or darker, so that the phenotype is affected at certain times of the year. Some roans darken over winter and only show their roaning in summer coat. Colours showing the most dramatic changes are the roans, duns, dilutes and chestnuts. The points of the horse and the soft parts may lighten completely, making identification difficult.

Exposure

Exposure to the elements has probably the greatest influence on coats in the short term. Swimming in seawater can improve a coat. Sunburn, sand and sweatburn cause bleaching and fading, whilst over-enthusiastic shampooing can dull a coat.

I knew a brown pony which relished the waterhole. Any hint of warmth in the summer and he would be drawn to it, to splash, roll and swim. This behaviour caused his coat to be bleached every year to a wishy-washy 'bay'. He was one of the rare exceptions to the rule that coat colour should be classified in summer.

Nutrition

Protein-rich food favours the accumulation of pigment. Horses of the red pigments are highly susceptible to changes in nutrition. Green spring feed, and oil seeds in particular, can have a drastic effect on the coats of these horses. For instance, it is generally known that large quantities of linseed can have a toxic effect on horses; in small quantities it gives the horse a darker, richer coat and diarrhoea. Lucerne, clover and pea hay can have the same effect.

Many a chestnut foal upon first change of coat goes very dark, fooling the owner into believing it is a liver chestnut. These 'false livers' are the result of rich mare's milk and good spring feed. Owners of palominos which tend to be light-coloured are often advised to feed lucerne and linseed fairly liberally. The reverse should never be practised, where a sooty horse is starved of all green feeds and given a low protein, poorly balanced diet to fade it out.

I am strongly against colour breed regulations which disallow colours too dark or too light. It tempts owners to try to falsify the colour for the sake of ego or registration. Far better to allow all shades that come within the genetic boundaries, and then have separate colour classes for 'ideal' colour. Colour should never become part of a led conformation (halter/material) class, for conformation ultimately suffers due to undue emphasis on the perfect colour. Such registries then lose credibility.

Poor nutrition in the form of malnutrition or dietary disturbance is a common destroyer of coat colour. Frequently, people who rescue a horse from near-starvation express delight in its change of colour once it is sleek and round.

Parasites

Hand in hand with nutrition go parasites both internal and external, which can effectively sap a horse's health, resulting in death from a variety of diseases. Parasites cause anaemia and general debility, resulting in poor bloom and coat colour. A zero egg count from the veterinary surgeon is the best way for an owner to ensure a worm-free horse, and iron/mineral supplementation is warranted until a zero egg count is obtained. Any coat will look wishy-washy if the horse is not in good health. A horse can never be a good horse if it cannot perform at its best. I am sure this is the real meaning behind the old saying, 'A good horse is never a bad colour'.

Hormones

Some colours are influenced by hormones to darken up or become more iridescent; in the case of the Appaloosa, there is an inherited component which allows males to colour up more readily than females of the same genotype. Hormones are directly influenced by diet, in particular by the fats in oils and seeds and the chlorophyll in fresh green grass. Stallions and in-foal mares are sleeker due to their levels of hormones.

Disease and metabolic disturbance

The effect of disease or metabolic disturbance will be self-evident by lack of energy, poor bloom or general failure to thrive. If disease or metabolic upset is suspected, have the horse's blood analysed so an effective management program can be initiated.

Six months on clean fresh pasture sprinkled with a few 'weeds' and herbs is often the cheapest and most effective longstanding cure.

GENERAL MANAGEMENT

Your horse's good coat is therefore dependent on your attitude towards its health. It is unusual for a horse to be genetically insipid in colour, just as it is rare for a horse to keep a perfect show coat out in the paddock with no help from you.

Warmth and protection from the elements in the form of a well-fitting canvas rug in winter (New Zealand rug with leg straps and tail flap) and a light summer ripstop rug on hot days, will keep the hair lying down and clean. A good protein diet of spring grass, irrigated pasture, or substitute

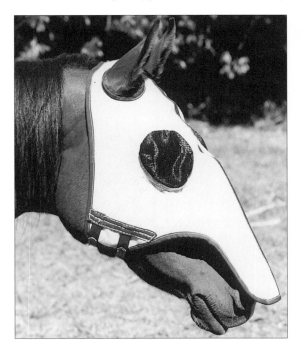

ABOVE: *New Zealand rug and hood*
LEFT: *Protective device for horses which suffer unduly from photosensitivity (courtesy Mylor Horse rugs)*

The same chestnut pony in spring (top) and winter coat (left)

Palomino with sabino characteristics showing faded neck where body has been rugged and neck exposed.

Tammy, a black buckskin in summer coat. This same pony is shown in winter coat on page 37

The same palomino pony in winter (top) and spring coat (bottom)

Four photos of the same pony, Caringal Isabel, registered Australian Pony and Australian Miniature, taken over several years. Note the degree to which the coat colour changes over time, due to environment (diet) and age (Photo A shows her when she is youngest, followed by B, C and D). Caringal Isabel was registered as palomino, but is a genuine taffy. The dark head (top left) indicates she is not sooty palomino, and the lightness on the side of the head (bottom right) indicates she is not liver with light mane and tail

balanced hand feeding, will suffice to produce a healthy horse. Don't overlook regular teeth care and parasite control.

The horse's coat is simply a reflection of its inner health. No amount of grooming will produce a top coat if the horse doesn't have inner health. I know a man who is allergic to horses and never touches one with a brush, yet the coats on his horses are outstanding; proof enough that it is not grooming that puts the shine on a horse. Notice too, that I have not mentioned stabling. Stabling may provide necessary protection for pink-skinned horses. Stables are certainly an advantage, especially in winter, when a light program for hair shedding can be initiated for early shows. However, stables are not essential; many of today's champions are prepared straight from the paddock (ours included).

I am intrigued by some of the latest showring fads—putting black boot polish well up the legs of a bay or grey horse, 'blacking' the white tail of a

grey, bleaching out black spots on palominos, or putting black hair dye through black manes and tails. Perhaps we should put more white on pintos, or draw thick black lines down the backs of our buckskins!

One famous false colour is the 'Condy's crystal chestnut'. 'A good horse is never a bad colour' should never be interpreted to mean that dark colours are good, and light colours bad.

For years this is how a 'good colour' has been interpreted, hence many old-timer judges will still refuse to place a palomino, a roan, or worse still, a pinto! Any colour breed owner knows that this prejudice still exists. Because of such colour blindness, most colour breed owners prefer to compete within their own breed group rather than in open competition.

Let's put the emphasis in judging away from colour and back to where it should be — performance.

24

QUESTIONS & ANSWERS

Q: Will homozygous (To^TTo^T) tobianos have more white than heterozygotes (To^TTo^+)?
A: No distinction can be made between the two.

Q: What are my chances of getting a homozygous tobiano when I breed two tobiano horses?
A: 25 per cent if the parents are heterozygous (rule 4, line 4, page 13);
50 per cent if one parent is homozygous (rule 2, line 2, page 13);
100 per cent if both parents are homozygous (rule 1, line 1, page 13).

Q: Has lethal white ever been reported in tobiano crosses?
A: Only where there is traceable overo breeding. The parents are in fact tobero.

Q: The overo stallion I wish to breed my overo mare to has never produced a lethal white foal. Will I risk getting a lethal white?
A: Yes. Statistically, one in four matings of your mare to this stallion will be a lethal white foal. However, you may get it first up, or not at all.

Q: Are mostly white overos more likely to produce lethal white than minimally marked ones?
A: No. Lethal white can also come from incomplete overos. All overos have the same 25 per cent chance of producing lethal white when bred together.

Q: Is the pinto a white horse with coloured patches or vice versa?
A: The latter. The pinto is a coloured horse with a white spotting pattern gene superimposed over genes for normal base colour.

Q: What base-coloured mares will give me the highest colour percentage from my Paint stallion?
A: None. As colour must come from the sire when breeding to solid mares, it makes no difference whether the mares are bay, brown, black or chestnut. However, due to unknown influences, probably non-genetic, it is possible that in borderline cases more white may show on a chestnut than a bay, brown or black, perhaps just enough to go 'above the line' and qualify as a Paint horse.

Q: Will homozygous (G^GG^G) greys whiten out with age more quickly than heterozygotes (G^GG^+)?
A: No evidence is available to suggest this to be the case.

Q: Will homozygous greys have a higher incidence of melanoma than heterozygotes?
A: As there is double the opportunity for one of the grey alleles to be linked to the melanoma gene, this is liable to be true.

Q: Can I breed out melanoma in a line of grey horses by changing the base colour I mate them to?
A: No; as melanoma may be linked to the greying gene, you must change the grey horses you are using to greys of another bloodline that appears free of melanoma.

Q: Why does the dilute gene whiten out the mane and tail of the palomino?
A: It is suggested that C^{cr} acts more strongly on the brown pigmentation of the mane and tail than on the red/yellow pigmentation of the body, but no-one really knows.

Q: Can blood markings occur on non-greys?
A: No. The dark patches that are sometimes observed on normal-coloured horses are just that, patches, or more commonly, smut marks.

Q: My grey Thoroughbred, which has large light patches on her, has been put in foal to a chestnut stallion. Can she produce a pinto?
A: No; the patches are very common on grey and, in fact, all grey Thoroughbreds trace back to a horse called The Tetrarch who was covered in light spots and patches. However, his skin was dark all over. These markings, known as 'watermarks', are not an unusual part of the greying process. They are in no way allied to pinto or spotted patterns.

Q: I am breeding my chestnut mare to a palomino stallion. Do I risk getting a dappled palomino if the mare has grey ancestors too close?
A: No, the two are not allied. If your mare does not have dapples in good coat condition, you are unlikely to get a foal with dapples.

Q: I have a four-year-old mare that is a cross between an Appaloosa and a Quarter Horse and she only has a few minor spots (almost like dabs with a paintbrush) on one shoulder. Someone told me that spots or changes in her coat could take place for up to five years. Is this true?
A: You do not say whether she has the characteristics of the Appaloosa in addition to the spots. This is essential. Without mottled skin, white sclera or striped hooves she is just another horse with unidentified spots. Chances are she does show characteristics, and she will continue to colour up. Appaloosas can become unrecognisable from year to year, well after their fifth year. One thing is true. If they haven't exhibited a pronounced pattern, such as leopard or spotted blanket early on, then these patterns will not emerge later. Typically, emerging colour is in the form of frosting or 'roaning' of the base coat, with some concentration on the hindquarters. Dark rarely emerges. These Appaloosas rarely ever seem 'finished' in their coat patterns.

Q: Why does my bay Appaloosa with spotted blanket have both black and red spots?
A: There is conjecture over this point, but the black will usually be over the hips and the red spots lower down. This indicates that the base coat is bay with a lot of black through the coat, as seen in a lot of dappled mahogany bays.

Q: I bred my buckskin mare to a black stallion and I suspect the foal is a dilute black. Can I register it?
A: Some buckskin groups accept the black buckskin by classification. If you suspect you have a black buckskin foal, take the precaution of photographing it before it changes its foal coat so you can substantiate your belief. The breed societies cannot be expected to prove colour identity for you. The onus is on you to submit all the facts to the best of your ability. They will look at each horse on its individual merits.

Q: My chestnut mare has much white ticking through her coat, and the chestnut stallion I wish to use does too. They have a common grandsire which is grey. If I breed to this stallion could I get a grey throwback or should I avoid inbreeding altogether?
A: You can't get a throwback because grey is dominant. It doesn't skip generations. The fact that the sire and dam are both chestnut means the greying gene is not present. It cannot be regained until and unless you breed her back to a grey stallion, and even then you may not get a grey. Inbreeding is not something that needs to be avoided. It is more important that you choose the best individuals, regardless of colour or their relationship to each other.

Q: Judges are often putting remarks on my dressage test pertaining to my brown horse's crookedness, which my instructor and I attribute to the blaze which runs off to one side. How can I overcome this?
A: This is not an uncommon problem. One very prominent three-day eventer in this country had a horse with a twisted blaze. He used to attract comments such as 'carries his head to one side' but black boot polish soon fixed that.

The Australian Stock Horse Society have a website to provide further information on Australian Stock Horses: **http://www.ashs.com.au/**

If you have a specific question you wish answered, please send A\$25 (overseas A\$30), a colour photo of your horse and self-addressed return envelope to:
Jeanette Gower
Box 822
Mt Barker SA 5251
Australia
Fax: (61) 08 8537 5033
Email: chalani@telstra.easymail.com.au
Website: http://members.xoom.com/chalani

25

ON BREEDING HORSES

In each Breed Society there are many breeders, but very few are true breeders. Only a small fraction of members strive continually to breed the very best type of animal and to improve all their stock. Others merely try to produce pure-bred progeny. This results only in an increase in the numbers of a breed, not in improvement. Surely an owner of horses who breeds a foal or two each year should ask himself the question, 'Am I trying to produce better foals?' The answer would have to be 'No' in many cases, because each year the same stallion is used on the same mares although the foals produced are not very useful or are, at best, ordinary.

If a person wants to keep horses, he should do so, but few foals should be bred. When replacements are required they should come from a reputable true breeder. Too many owners feel that they are in some way being cheated if they do not get a foal from their favourite mare. This mare should only be bred from if she fulfils all other criteria for suitability as a broodmare. It is not just a matter of breeding—it is a matter of accumulating more horses that must be fed, handled, educated and usually sold to make way for the next.

Every owner of horses should consider seriously whether he is a horse keeper or horse breeder; he should choose between improving the progeny or remaining an owner who ceases trying to propagate the breed.

In the 1930s an article appeared in a United States breed newsletter (author unknown) from which I quote a small section:

From the years of extensive study the author has done on the subject to date, and continues to do, I have come to the conclusion that most horse breeders have absolutely no breeding program, no rhyme nor reason for their efforts, and the only way they ever get an outstanding individual is by accident! I've studied some breeding programmes in depth and the more I studied these people's programmes the more convinced I have become that most of them still are breeding horses in the Dark Ages manner.

Most of them when pinned down to direct questions as to 'why' they produced what they have, will simply say it is because they owned the two parents, they 'liked' the mate they selected, or the stallion was just down the road. One might call it not an increase in horse population, but an increase in horse pollution!

If breeders stopped to think what they are breeding for, if it is simply to produce a foal, or if it is with a sincere purpose in mind and a basis for that mating, fewer grade horses would be produced. But those you would find would be much more extensively pedigreed, of much greater quality, and in much greater demand.

In a thumbnail survey recently of 100 horsebreeders in an area with 'known' reputation, I found only two that had any scientific basis for their breeding programme. That left 98 per cent breeding in a haphazard fashion.

These are strong words but I don't doubt that 60 years later they still apply in spite of the fact that modern breeders now have the added benefit of the science of genetics to help them.

Australia is a case in point. In fact, I go so far as to say that the excellent work done by Australian breeders in the past to breed The Best Horse In The World is being undone by the damage caused by the reckless chasing of imported and exotic bloodlines at the expense of our proven lines.

The science of breeding animals up to a high standard is fascinating. It cannot be learned in a short time, by reading the odd book or two, or by listening to a few chance remarks; it can be learned only through experience, backed up by discussion with those more experienced, as well as reading as much as possible on the subject. Many things must be considered, many difficulties arise, and it is one of the quickest ways to lose money! After breeding a few foals, most newcomers realise that it is cheaper to buy what they want (and preferably at an early age if the price is not to be too high).

But if the breeder's efforts are successful they lead to much pleasure and satisfaction. Even the most successful breeder, however, is rarely entirely satisfied and he will strive to achieve better results. (This is one reason why his good stock will come on the market.)

To be a successful horse breeder one must be an all-round horseman, for the breeder must be prepared to ride his stock to put them to the test. He must have a thorough knowledge of husbandry, nutrition, reproductive physiology, bloodlines, genetics and conformation. This is acquired only through years of research, good health to do the enormous amount of physical work, business skills in record keeping, advertising and marketing, and of course, providing good customer service. He must do all this himself, or have an endless cheque book to pay expert staff to do so.

He should be prepared to put his stock before the public eye for promotion, and to sustain the inevitable criticism. Horsemen are notorious for their steadfast belief that if they love their horses, buyers will beat a path to their doorstep to buy. Any difficulty a breeder experiences in finding suitable buyers for his youngsters should indicate that a reassessment of the suitability of such horses is in order. If the animals don't measure up, and the promotion is not ongoing, this will be reflected in the lack of a ready market.

Some breeders look but never see. They are continually knocking other breeders' horses, especially those who are fortunate to capture the ribbons. Perhaps the winning breeders are more selective in their choice and give more time and dedication to competing with their horses. If they are winning with horses that are not your type, it is time to look at your own type in a very searching way.

There are horses which will never produce progeny likely to be an improvement on themselves. This is particularly true of some stallions, so if the owner's aim (as one hopes) is to improve his stock, it is a waste of time, effort and money to continue using such an animal. It may be difficult sentimentally to cull such a horse, but a genuine intention to improve one's horses necessitates a hardening of heart by gelding or pensioning off. It is far too often that one hears the unsurprising remark that such and such a stallion has not left foals of any note. On examination one usually finds that the animal in question is underbred and lacking the quality required or, less often, is a better than usual representative of an inferior bloodline. There is no substitute for a top pedigree of names proven in open, high level competition.

It is astonishing how few buyers other than racehorse buyers really study pedigrees in depth and take an intelligent interest in the breeding of horses. Yet this is the breeder's most valuable tool. Top bloodlines must be used; it is not sufficient to select a stallion simply because he traces to some well-known individual. It is also surprising the number of studs that keep mares that have not even been broken in, or that have failed to perform. Buyers would be well advised to steer clear of such studs. All the names in a pedigree should be top class and from recognised breeders. This of course will cost money, so if the price is low one must question the merit of the horse under consideration.

A proven breeding horse will only come cheaply if it is aged (usually 15 years or over), but a breeder is far better to acquire such a horse than to compromise on quality and pedigree. Breeders should choose mares similar in appearance. A true breeder's stud will have a bunch of mares obviously bred and selected with care, of outstanding pedigree and proven performance, all showing similar good type and breed characteristics. The stallion cannot be expected to do it all. In fact, when inspecting a stallion I will always inspect his mares, for the quality of his mates will indicate the value placed on him by mare owners, and therefore the quality of the resulting foals. No owner will send a top quality mare to a substandard stallion.

Without dedication to the goal of improvement with each generation, a horseperson should never take on the art and science of breeding horses. Without knowledge to persevere through fads and fashions, and the whims of nature which are inevitable, only disappointment can result. The true thinking breeder understands all this and the proof is in the top quality animals which are consistently produced and which have a ready market.

BREEDING FOR COLOUR

I still find joy and amazement in the birth of a foal. After 25 years experience, the thrill of seeing last year's planned matings come to fruition in the new-born is still no less exciting to me. No matter how 'planned' a mating, there is always the possibility of something unusual or unpredicted occurring—the foal that was never meant to be, or the foal that exceeded all expectations. This is what keeps the breeder's dream alive—the search for the elusive 'perfect' horse that is each person's ideal, and that money can't buy.

However, it may come as a surprise that I have never bred for colour. Colour inheritance has always been an interest for me, but I have never planned a mating to try to obtain, or avoid, a certain colour. The Australian Stock Horse has always been my favourite and no colours are barred. Theoretically, if we chose to, my husband and I could breed any colour we wanted, or which we thought would be commercially more attractive. However, we have always stuck rigidly to the belief that it is more important to breed a good horse, and that 'a good horse is never a bad colour'. I have seen time and again attempts by breeders to breed only for colour and, before long, type and temperament are sacrificed.

Many breeders are attracted to colour breeding in the belief that certain colours will sell at higher prices, yet they fail to realise that to stay in the horse business they must also market the inevitable non-coloured produce. To stay in the horse business, it is the overall average price of the breeder's stock which counts, not the occasional well-publicised high or record price.

The non-coloured progeny must be good horses in their own right to allow for reliable sales and to keep average prices up. I cannot impress enough that breeding horses is a very expensive hobby, and few people make a go of it without supporting incomes and considerable knowledge.

I don't believe in good luck. Our success as breeders has come from setting goals, observing, listening, planning, patience and hard work. You can do the same if you want it badly enough.

Be open-minded enough to listen to those who are successful and smart enough to distinguish these from those who just like to talk a lot.

So good planning and make your own good luck!

APPENDIX

COLOUR EFFECTS

TABLE A: **Action of colour alleles of the horse** (CONTINUES OVER PAGE)

Series	Locus	Allele	Effect of the allele
Agouti	A	A^+	Light (primitive) bay
		A^A	Restricts eumelanin (black) to the points, mane and tail, bay
		A^t	Removes eumelanin pigment from the soft parts, brown
		A^a	No restriction, full eumelanin production, black
Mottled	Ap	Ap^{Ap}	Creates spotted characteristics, mottling
		Ap^+	The normal allele, solid, no effect
Chocolate	B	B^+	Black pigmentation, the normal allele
		B^b	Chocolate pigmentation with pinkish brown skin
Cremello	Cr	C^{cr}	Cremello dilution of pigmentation
		C^+	Full colour, the normal allele
Champagne	Ch	Ch^C	Rare champagne dilution of pigmentation
		Ch^+	Full colour, the normal allele
Dun	D	D^+	Native dun
		D^D	The dunning dilution of pigmentation
		D^+	Full colour, the normal allele
Extension	E	E^D	Creates dominant black
		E^+	Extends eumelanin production, black
		E^e	Causes production of phaeomelanin (red), chestnut
Flaxen	F	F^+	The normal allele, no effect
		F^f	Creates flaxen mane and tail in E^e horses
Grey	G	G^G	Creates progressive greying
		G^+	The normal allele, no effect
Marbling	M	M^M	Causes marble markings
		M^+	The normal allele, no effect
White markings	N	N^+	Prevents white markings, no white, the wild allele
		N^n	Allows white markings to occur
Overo	O	O^O	Causes pigment loss in the form of overo pinto
		O^+	The normal allele, no effect
Pangaré	P	P^+	The normal allele, no effect
		P^p	Creates a pronounced muzzle ring, and light cast on the under-side of the body, pangaré
Roan	Rn	Rn^{Rn}	Creates an admixture of light and dark hairs, roan
		Rn^+	The normal allele, no effect
Sabino	Sb	Sb^S	Causes pigment loss in the form of sabino white markings, only in the presence of N^n.
		Sb^+	The normal allele, normal white markings in the presence of N^n.

TABLE A: Action of colour alleles of the horse (CONTINUED)

Series	Locus	Allele	Effect of the allele
Snowcap	*Sc*	Sc^S	Causes pigment loss in the form of snowcap spotting, in the presence of Ap^{Ap}, blanket, etc.
		Sc^+	The normal allele, no effect
Dark spots	*Sd*	Sd^S	Causes dark spots in the presence of Ap^{Ap}
		Sd^+	The normal allele, no effect
Snowflake	*Sn*	Sn^S	Causes white spotting in the presence of Ap^{Ap}, snowflake
		Sn^+	The normal allele, no effect
Varnish	*Sv*	Sv^S	Causes silvering in the presence of Ap^{Ap}, varnish
		Sv^+	The normal allele, no effect
Splashed white	*Spl*	Spl^S	Causes pigment loss in the form of splashed white pinto
		Spl^+	The normal allele, no effect
Sooty	*Sty*	Sty^S	Creates an intermingling of dark hairs through the coat, seasonal dapples
		Sty^+	The normal allele, no effect
Tobiano	*To*	To^T	Causes pigment loss in the form of tobiano pinto
		To^+	The normal allele, no effect
White	*W*	W^W	Causes pigment loss in hair and skin, but not eyes, dominant white
		W^+	The normal allele, no effect
Taffy	*Z*	Z^Z	The taffy dilution of pigmentation silver dapple
		Z^+	The normal allele, no effect

Table B Trihybrid cross—$A^AA^aD^DD^dE^+E^e$ *sire* × $A^AA^aD^DD^dE^+E^e$ *dam* (yellow dun × yellow dun)

sire dam	*ADE*	*Ade*	*AdE*	*Ade*	*aDE*	*adE*	*aDe*	*ade*
ADE	AADDEE	AADDEe	AADdEE	AADdEe	AaDDEE	AaDdEE	AaDDEe	AaDdEe
Ade	AADDEe	AADDee	AADdEe	AADdee	AaDDEe	AaDdEe	AaDDee	AaDdee
AdE	AADdEE	AADdEe	AAddEE	AAddEe	AaDdEE	AaddEE	AaDdEe	AaddEe
Ade	AADdEe	AADdee	AAddEe	Aaddee	AaDdEe	AaddEe	AaDdee	Aaddee
aDE	AaDDEE	AaDDEe	AaDdEE	AaDdEe	aaDDEE	aaDdEE	aaDDEe	aaDdEe
adE	AaDdEE	AaDdEe	AaddEE	AaddEe	aaDdEE	aaddEE	aaDdEe	aaddEe
aDe	AaDDEe	AaDDee	AaDdEe	AaDdee	aaDDEe	aaDdEe	aaDDee	aaDdee
ade	AaDdEe	AaDdee	AaddEe	Aaddee	aaDdEe	aaddEe	aaDdee	aaddee

Result: 64 combinations; ratio of offspring 27:9:9:9:3:3:3:1 or 42.2% *A_D_E_*, 14.06% *A_D_ee*, 14.06% *A_ddE_*, 14.06% *aaD_E_*, 4.68% *A_ddee*, 4.68% *aaD_ee*, 4.68% *aaddE_*, and 1.56% *aaddee*.

TABLE C COLOUR DICTIONARY OF GENOTYPES

$A^+\_C^+C^+D^dD^dE^eE^e$	Light chestnut	$A^+\_C^+C^+D^D\_E^eE^e$	Peach dun
$A^A\_C^+C^+D^dD^dE^eE^e$	Red chestnut	$A^A\_C^+C^+D^D\_E^eE^e$	Copper dun
$A^t\_C^+C^+D^dD^dE^eE^e$	Standard chestnut	$A^t\_C^+C^+D^D\_E^eE^e$	Red dun
$A^aA^aC^+C^+D^dD^dE^eE^e$	Liver chestnut	$A^aA^aC^+C^+D^D\_E^eE^e$	Liver dun
$A^+\_C^+C^+D^dD^dE^+\_$	Light bay	$A^+\_C^+C^+D^D\_E^+\_$	Silver dun
$A^A\_C^+C^+D^dD^dE^+\_$	Bay	$A^A\_C^+C^+D^D\_E^+\_$	Yellow dun
$A^t\_C^+C^+D^dD^dE^+\_$	Brown	$A^t\_C^+C^+D^D\_E^+\_$	Mouse dun
$A^aA^aC^+C^+D^dD^dE^+\_$	Black	$A^aA^aC^+C^+D^D\_E^+\_$	Grullo or blue dun
$A^A\_C^+C^{cr}D^dD^dE^eE^e$	Golden palomino	$A^A\_C^+C^{cr}D^D\_E^eE^e$	Claybank or palomino dun
$A^t\_C^+C^{cr}D^dD^dE^eE^e$	Seasonal palomino	$A^t\_C^+C^{cr}D^D\_E^eE^e$	Claybank dun
$A^aA^aC^+C^{cr}D^dD^dE^eE^e$	Dark palomino	$A^aA^aC^+C^{cr}D^D\_E^eE^e$	Claybank dun
$A^A\_C^+C^{cr}D^dD^dE^+\_$	Golden buckskin	$A^A\_C^+C^{cr}D^D\_E^+\_$	Composite yellow dun
$A^t\_C^+C^{cr}D^dD^dE^+\_$	Mouse buckskin	$A^t\_C^+C^{cr}D^D\_E^+\_$	Composite yellow dun
$A^aA^aC^+C^{cr}D^dD^dE^+\_$	Black buckskin	$A^aA^aC^+C^{cr}D^D\_E^+\_$	Composite grullo

TABLE D COLOUR EFFECTS

Colours which are lethal when homozygous
Overo (white foal syndrome/lethal white)
Roan
Splashed white
Dominant white

Colours which are true breeding when crossed to one another
Chestnut × chestnut
Few-spot × few-spot
Pseudo-albino × pseudo-albino

Colours which are never true breeding

Buckskin	Palomino
Dominant white	Roan
Overo	Splashed white

Colours which are true breeding when homozygous

Bay	Sabino
Dun	Taffy
Grey	Tobiano

TABLE E COLOUR FAMILIES

Base colours/hard colours
Chestnut, black, brown and bay

In the past these have been called 'intense' colours.

Thoroughbred colours
Chestnut, black, brown, bay and grey

Full colours
All C^+C^+ horses: chestnut, black, brown, bay, grey, roan, dun and taffy

Solid colours
All full colours, single dilutes (C^+C^{cr}), double dilutes ($C^{cr}C^{cr}$) and champagnes (Ch^C): chestnut, black, brown, bay, grey, roan, dun, taffy, buckskin, palomino, cremello, perlino and champagne

Coloured
All pied (pinto) horses (To^T, O^o, Spl^S, and Sb^S) and spotted (leopard complex) patterns.

TABLE F ALTERNATIVE COLOUR NAMES

Many colours are known by alternative names in their local area, but their use may cause difficulties as they are neither wide ranging nor well defined. Listed below are the preferred names and some alternatives you may hear that are best avoided, except where clearly defined.

BAY—mahogany, bronze, wolf bay, sable bay, blood; Icelandic—jarpur, Dutch—bruin.
BIRDCATCHER TICK—armabi, hare-ticked.
BROKEN COLOURED—parti-coloured, odd-coloured, coloured, painted, pinto.
BROWN—wolf brown, seal brown, bay.
BUCKSKIN—mouse, creamy with black points, dun.
CREMELLO—creme, blue-eyed cream, albino, cremolin, glass-eyed creamy.
CHESTNUT—sorrel, liver, chocolate, sandy, red, wolf chestnut, blonde sorrel, mud chestnut; Icelandic—rauour, Dutch—vos.
CLAYBANK—red dun, lemonsilla, palomino dun, yellow dun.
COON-TAILED TICK—rabicano, Cohn's stripes.
DORSAL STRIPE—donkey stripe, eel stripe, list, race, eel mark, lineback.
DUN—bayo, agouti, sable.
GREY—blue, white, salt and pepper, steel, silver, iron, rose.
GRULLO—blue dun, grey dun, mouse, slate, lobuno, lobo dun, grulla, crane, smoky.
LEG BARRINGS—tiger stripes, zebra marks.
LEMONSILLA—cactus chestnut, claybank, taffy.
CHAMPAGNE BLACK—lilac dun, dove dun.
MARBLE MARKINGS—cat-backed, lace markings.
MASK—nose rug, smudge face.
MEALY MUZZLE—muzzle ring, soft parts, toad face, coppernose, pangaré.
MOTTLED—pinkie syndrome, Appaloosa characteristics, corn spots, speckled, freckled.
OVERO—calico, paint, medicine hat, frame.
PALOMINO—cream, creamy with light mane and tail, Isabella, Ysabelle, golden, palomillo, sovereign creamy.
PINTO—piebald, skewbald, odd-coloured, broken-coloured, pintado.
RED DUN—muddy dun, apricot dun, peach dun, copper dun, yellow dun with dun mane and tail.
ROAN—blue, strawberry, silver, varnish, ticked, lavender.
SHOULDER STRIPE—wither list, donkey list, cross, donkey cross.
SABINO—bird egg, grizzle, grissle, rount, chubari, blotched, feathered, crop-out, blagden, splashed, high white, wild white.
SMOKY PERLINO—silver smoky.
SPECKLED—roan, lace-spotted.
SPOTTED—appaloosa, leopard, snowflake, blanket, snowcap, smutty, Bend Or spots.
TAFFY—silver dapple, vindott, chocolate palomino, crypto-palomino, chocolate flax, silver sorrel.
TICKING—flecking, roan, coon tail, birdcatcher tick, rabicano, armabi
TOBIANO—piebald, skewbald, broken-coloured, pied, targum.
TOTAL SOLID—self-coloured, whole-coloured, unmarked.
WHITE—camarillo, blanco.
YELLOW DUN—zebra dun.

GLOSSARY

alazan Chestnut horse with red points.

allele Alternative genes possible at a certain locus.

Appaloosa Spotted breed of horse developed in USA from foundation stock of the Nez Pearce Indian tribe.

Arabian Breed of pure-bred horse developed by the desert tribes of Arabia.

armabi A form of ticking. (*See* Chapter 13).

Australian Pony Registered breed of pony derived from Welsh, Timorese, Arab and Hackney blood, developed in Australia.

Australian Stock Horse Recognised breed of working horse in Australia derived from Thoroughbred, station and remount horses.

base colours Bay, brown, black or chestnut.

bay Yellow-red to reddish-brown body colour with black legs, mane and tail.

black Black all over except where faded due to weathering.

black type Names in a racehorse pedigree printed in bold type to indicate those horses so named are major stakeswinners.

blanket White, 'roan' or spotted patch on hindquarters.

blood markings Red or, less commonly, other coloured patches on a grey horse.

blue dun *See* grullo.

blue eye 1) Dark blue eye; 2) Common use collective term for glass, wall, or watch eye.

bordered A marking that has a rim of mixed or roaned hair around a solid-coloured centre; halo effect.

breeding stock 1) Foundation registry for progeny of fully registered parents that do not meet minimum colour requirements, so their bloodlines may still be recorded. Such horses may go on to produce fully registerable foals; 2) Horses used for breeding purposes, stallions and broodmares.

broken colour Any parti-coloured horse with pink skin underlying the white hair, as in pied and spotted horses.

brown Liver brown or black body colour with black legs, mane and tail, light soft parts; often included with bay.

buckskin A dilute colour ranging from cream, through yellow or orange, with black legs, mane and tail, resulting from the C^{cr} dilution.

by Horseman's terminology, short for 'sired by', always in reference to the stallion, never the mare.

chestnut 1) Various shades of red or brown, without black legs, mane or tail; 2) Horny growth on the inside of the legs.

chinspot White marking anywhere on the lower lip, chin or underjaw.

chocolate Specific term for rare chocolate-coloured horse with light brown skin and eyes.

chocolate flax A form of taffy.

CID Combined immunodeficiency syndrome, a recessive lethal disease of young Arabian horses, with similarities to AIDS.

claybank A dull yellowish colour, with tan, yellow or cream points, the dilute of red dun.

Clydesdale Scottish breed of draught horse, Australia's most popular draught breed.

co-dominant *See* incomplete inheritance.

Coffin Bay Pony Line of endangered feral ponies running in the Coffin Bay National Park, near Port Lincoln, South Australia.

Coldblood Any draught breed or cross, a heavily built horse used for heavy harness work.

colt Young male horse not yet of reproductive age.

conformation The structural shape and muscular form of the horse.

coronary band (or coronet) *See* diagram of parts of the horse, page 7.

cremello Off-white with pink skin and blue eyes.

cross breeding Crosses between different breeds.

crop-out Broken-coloured horse of solid-coloured parents.

cull To remove from the breeding herd by gelding, pensioning off, or putting back into work.

dapples Dark rings from coin- to fist-sized, usually seen on greys and taffies.

depigmentation Sporadic removal of pigment resulting in pink skin and white hair.

developmental noise Cellular and inter-uterine environmental influences affecting the developing foetus, not caused by genetic factors.

dilute 1) Genetic action resulting in a lightened colour; 2) A light body colour resulting from a dilution gene.

DNA Deoxyribonucleic acid; the chemical substance of heredity. Stored in the molecules that make up the core of the chromosomes.

dominant The ability of a gene to mask another so that its appearance never skips a generation.

dorsal stripe Dark line running down the spine of the horse.

double dilute Collective term for all colours homozygous for the C^{cr} gene.

dun A diluted body colour with prominent dorsal stripe, leg barring and face mask resulting from the D dilution.

epistatic Genetic action resulting in masking of genes of a different series or locus.

ermine spots Coloured spots on a white sock.

eumelanin Black pigmentation.

excessive white High white markings that spread above an arbitrary line drawn up by breed registries.

few-spot Spotting pattern, devoid of the usual number of spots, in Appaloosas and other breeds resulting in a mostly white horse.

filly Young female horse not yet of reproductive age.

Finnish paint *See* splashed white.

Fjord Pony Sturdy breed of dun pony developed in Norway.

flaxen Light colour, yellow or ivory; usually refers to the points.

flea-bitten speckled grey.

foal Young horse which has not yet been weaned, sometimes referred to as a 'colt' in US literature.

founder effect Look-alike populations as a result of the influence of one or a few foundation individuals.

full colour Bay, brown, black, chestnut, or grey.

gaited A horse that ambles, paces, racks or performs the running walk as in the Icelandic Pony and Tennessee Walking Horse. Some breeds do this naturally; others perform them artificially by heavy shoeing and other means. Artificial gaiting is not practised in Australia.

gene A unit of heredity located on the chromosomes.

genotype The genetic blueprint which governs the characteristics that can be replicated in the progeny.

gelding A castrated male horse of any age; also the act of gelding, or castration.

ghost markings Faint primitive markings, usually seen on foals, which tend to disappear with age.

grade horse Horse of mixed breeding.

grey Body colour which progressively whitens with age.

grullo A slate grey-dun colour characterised by smoky black face, points and dorsal stripe (Spanish: *grullo* = male, *grulla* = female).

halo effect *See* bordered.

heterozygous A pair of alleles which are not alike.

high white An excessively white marked horse.

homozygous A pair of alleles which are identical.

Hotblood Any breed derived primarily from Oriental sources such as Andalusian, Arabian, Barb, Thoroughbred.

hybrid 1) Cross of different species; 2) Genetic term to indicate crosses at different loci resulting in heterozygosity.

HYPP Hyperkalemic periodic paralysis, a dominant inherited muscle enzyme disorder which may cause stiffness, tremors and even death, but is usually well controlled by appropriate diet.

inbreeding The breeding of individuals closely related to one another.

incomplete inheritance Partial-dominance or co-dominance, where two alleles have an equal effect resulting in an intermediate phenotype.

incomplete or crypto-pinto A horse carrying a broken-coloured pattern gene such as tobiano or overo, but without qualifying body markings, often incorrectly registered as solid.

iridescence A shiny metallic glint of the coat.

lemonsilla A khaki yellow horse.

leopard Spotted horse with white background.

leopard complex Geneticists' collective term for all spotting patterns not pied.

lethal Causes death, either at birth, or later in the adult horse (delayed), or only under certain environmental conditions (partial).

lightning pattern Term used for ragged vertical white on an overo.

linebreeding A form of inbreeding to a common ancestor.

linkage Genes which are located on the same chromosome and tend to be inherited together.

locus A position on a chromosome occupied by

one of a gene series which controls a specific trait.

loud Bold markings, usually refers to large white markings.

mare Female horse of breeding age.

marble markings Progressive white speckling with age over the spine.

mask Dark colour down the bridge of the nose or face; but can be most of the face.

medicine hat An extensive white pinto with some colour remaining on the top half of the head.

melanocytes Cells that produce colour in the skin.

melanoma Benign clusters of pigment growths that affect some greys, not to be confused with true melanoma which is a form of skin cancer.

migration Slow change in position of spots, smuts or speckles, the change frequently obvious upon comparison of photographs.

mismark White or dark mark present from birth, but not of an inherited nature.

mottled 1) Spotted skin pigmentation about the face and genitalia; 2) Loose term for any regular pattern of dark, round spots.

multi-factorial (polygenic) The result of several groups of genes present simultaneously, at several loci, for example, modifier genes for white markings.

mutation Very rare, sudden appearance of a new gene not already in the breed.

muzzle ring Sharply delineated mealy, oatmeal colour running well up the muzzle.

odd-coloured Obsolete English term for a broken-coloured horse of more than two colours.

outback Australia's rugged interior of semi-desert and bushland.

out of Horseman's terminology, short for 'born out of the mare'; always refers to the dam, never the sire.

overo A dominant form of pied marking.

Paint Breed of pinto horse derived from Thoroughbred and Quarter Horse, developed in the USA.

palomino A golden horse with white mane and tail.

pangaré Genetic action creating muzzle ring and lightening out of the lower body and soft parts.

pedigree Charted history of a horse's ancestors (usually three of four generations), like a family tree.

penetrance The proportion of animals of a given genotype which exhibit the trait in the phenotype.

perlino Ivory-white with pink skin, cream or coffee coloured legs, mane and tail. (see also smoky perlino).

phaeomelanin Red/yellow pigmentation.

phenotype An individual's measurable or observable characteristics.

photosensitivity Intolerance of sunlight, an allergic reaction.

pied A horse with white patches over its body, except leopard complex.

pinto Collective term for all types of pied horses.

Pinto Registry for pinto-coloured horses of any breed, except draught and gaited breeds.

pleiotropic effects Several effects under the control of a single gene.

points The mane, tail and lower legs, sometimes including eartips and rims of the nostrils.

pseudo-albino 1) Collective term for a perlino and cremello; 2) Any double dilute.

primitive markings Collective term for dorsal stripe, leg barring and all secondary dun characteristics. *See* chapter 9, page 38.

Przewalski's Horse Mongolian wild horse, last of the original wild horse species.

pure-bred No crosses outside a specific population, strain or recognised breed. Usually refers to pedigreed stock carefully bred over many generations.

Quarter Horse Breed of quarter-mile sprint racehorse and working cattle horse developed in the USA from Thoroughbred and ranch horses.

rabicano Brush-tailed, ticked horse, the coon-tailed tick.

recessive The ability of a gene to be masked by another, and be passed on unknown into future generations.

red dun A dun with light red body colour, and darker red mask and points.

registration Identification certification by a breed association or registry upon fulfilment of entry requirements.

repigmentation Sporadic return of colour in a pink-skinned horse, resulting in spots or patches of colour.

roan Permanent intermingling of white and dark hairs over the body, but not on the points.

rount Loose term for a speckled horse appearing blue or pink.

ruano Chestnut horse with light points.

sabino A form of pied marking.

sclera The outer ring of the eye, may be white.

seal brown A particular shade of brown, defined as a black horse with red or yellow soft parts.

seal point Dark or light brown points as distinct from black points.

self-coloured A horse of the same colour all over (white markings excepted).

series A group of genes which influences a particular hereditary trait sited on a particular locus.

Shetland Pony Diminutive breed of horse which traces in pure lineage to ponies native to the Shetland Isles.

silver dapple American term for taffy.

smuts Black or liver spots on a normal-coloured horse.

snowcap White blanket or larger, seen in spotted horses.

snowflake White spots seen in spotted horses.

soft parts The 'ticklish' areas: flanks, elbows, girth, hams, inner legs, muzzle, behind the eyes, base of ears.

solid colour A full-coloured horse not broken by patches of white over its body.

sooty Heavy concentration of black or liver hairs intermingled throughout the base coat, often forming dapples.

sorrel Light chestnut.

spear inverted V-point white marking on the top of a sock.

splashed white A rare form of pied marking.

spotted 1) Covered in spots, such as in the Appaloosa; 2) collective term used by geneticists for pied markings and the leopard complex.

stallion Entire male horse of reproductive age.

station horse Australian term for ranch or farmbred cattle horse, 'off the station', usually of Thoroughbred descent.

stockman Australian term for rider who works cattle or sheep; cowboy.

taffy A dilute colour: 1) Chocolate with dapples and light mane and tail; 2) Orange body with tan legs and light mane and tail.

Tarpan European wild horse of dun colour, now extinct.

texturing Changes in layers of hair that may be distinguished by touch.

Thoroughbred Breed of pure-bred horse developed in England for racing, and descending from only three stallions.

throwback Reappearance of a recessive trait which has been hidden and unknowingly passed on from both sire and dam, giving the impression that the trait has been caused by the influence of a single distant ancestor.

ticking White hairs intermingled throughout a solid coat; flecking.

Timor Pony Ponies imported to Australia during Colonial times from the island of Timor, fine-coated, sturdy and more like small horses than ponies.

tobiano The most common form of pied marking.

tostado Chestnut horse with brown points.

total solid Without any white markings.

tying-up syndrome Excess nitrogen in the urine with associated destruction of skeletal muscle.

varnish Coat pattern somewhat like roan seen in spotted horses.

vindott Icelandic term for taffy.

Waler Australian army remount horse, primarily of Thoroughbred blood, shipped from New South Wales for service in the British colonies, especially to India, Egypt and South Africa. It acquired outstanding reputation worldwide as the greatest horse of its time under the most extreme conditions. The Waler has had a major influence on the Australian Stock Horse breed.

Warmblood Any cross of Hotblood with Coldblood. More recently the term has come to mean registered descendants of horses recognised in the various Warmblood Stud Books of Europe.

watermarks White or light spots or patches without underlying pink skin on a grey horse.

wheaten-skinned Skin of a pink or pumpkin colour.

white All-white coat with pink skin and normal eyes.

whole-coloured A horse without white markings anywhere, totally solid.

wild form The native allele (for each locus) of an animal in its natural environment. Domestication has meant the wild form may be rare in some species.

zebra dun Yellow dun.

zebra stripes Prominent transverse lines on the knees and hocks.

Recommended Reading

Leicester, Charles (1957) *Bloodstock Breeding*. J A Allen and Co., London.

Tesio, F. (1958) *Breeding the Racehorse*. J. A. Allen and Co., London.

Bogart and Jones (1973) *Genetics of the Horse*. Caballus Publishers, Colorado, USA.

Green B.K. (1974) *The Colour of Horses*. Northland Press, Flagstaff, Arizona, USA.

Geurts, R. (1977) *Hair Colour in the Horse* (translated by A. Dent). J.H. Allen and Co., London.

Miller, R.W. (no date) *Appaloosa coat colour inheritance*. Appaloosa Horse Club, Moscow, Idaho.

Equine Research Foundation (1978) *Equine Genetics and Selection Procedures*. Dallas, Texas.

Hultgren, B.V. (1982) 'Ileocolonic aganglionosis in white progeny of overo spotted horses', *Journal of American Veterinary Medicine Association*, vol. 180, no. 3.

Sponenberg, D.P. and Beaver, B.V. (1983) *Horse Colour*. A & M University Press, College Station, Texas.

Woolf, C.M. (1989) 'Multifactorial Inheritance of White Facial Markings in the Arabian Horse', *Journal of Heredity*, vol. 80.

Evans, Borton, Hintz & Van Vleck (1990) *The Horse* (2nd edition). W.H. Freeman and Co, New York.

Sponenberg, D.P. (1990) 'Inheritance of the Leopard Complex of Spotting Patterns in Horse', *Journal of Heredity*, vol. 81.

North, E. (1992) *Breeding for Colour*. Northfork Press, Mississippi.

Woodbridge Mulder, C. (1994) 'The White Arabians of Australia', *Arabian Visions Magazine*, Nov.-Dec.

*Bowling, A. (1996) *Horse Genetics*. CAB International, Oxford University Press, Cary, North Carolina.

*Sponenberg, D.P. (1996) *Equine Colour Genetics*. Iowa State University Press, Ames, Iowa.

Haun, Marianna (1997) *The X Factor: The Relationship between Inherited Heart Size and Racing Performance*, The Russell Meerdink Co. Ltd, Neenah WI 54956 USA.

Ramsey, David (1997) *Rocky Mountain Horse Eyes Provide Comparative Study to Similar Human Ocular Conditions*, Veterinary Medical Centre, Michigan State University, East Lansing MI 48824.

*These two references are highly recommended.

INDEX